COMMON SENSE NOT REQUIRED

Idiots Designing Cars & Hybrid Vehicles

Includes: How to find a good mechanic.

My Career with Chrysler

By
Evan Boberg

ISBN: 1-4140-4079-2 (e-book)
ISBN: 1-4140-4077-6 (Paperback)
ISBN: 1-4140-4078-4 (Dust Jacket)

Library of Congress Control Number: 2004090521

This book is printed on acid free paper.

Printed in the United States of America
Bloomington, IN

1stBooks – rev. 01/22/04

For my wife,

Anne.

Acknowledgments

My wife Anne for her encouragement, patience and copy editing skills. My sister, Gina Darlington for her enthusiasm and editing help. Also my Father-in-law, Harry Glick and neighbor Adene Scott for editing suggestions. The Internet for it's abundance of information. And Chrysler for nearly 12 years of a really fun job!

Table Of Contents

INTRODUCTION

I used to love cars. So much so, that after graduation from college, I moved to Detroit hoping to design cars.

Cars move humans around much faster than even the fittest on a bicycle. Airplanes go even faster, but I have to "drive" to an airport to see one. A car is parked at every house. The car in my view is the most important machine influencing our lives. It can carry all your stuff and take you almost anywhere you want to go whenever you want.

This is miraculous to me; that mankind has devised devices which so extraordinarily increase man's ability to move around quickly. I had the illusion it took very smart people to design and build cars. I thought I was smart enough to do it too.

I obtained employment with American Motors Corporation (AMC) in 1986, which merged with Chrysler Corporation in 1987. After 12 years in the auto industry, I came to the conclusion that smart people weren't required, and moreover not valued in the industry. The industry flourished despite what I call a "proliferation of idiots." Considering myself one of the very smart ones, and not being valued by the corporation, I resigned and moved back to my childhood home.

In my last position at Chrysler, I was one of the originators of computer simulation of hybrid vehicles. Until I left the corporation, the majority of the simulation work was done by me. With hybrid vehicles currently on the market, my experiences and views about them are quite timely.

Since leaving Chrysler, I've had many conversations with relatives and friends in which I have shared stories about my years in Detroit. These stories are often humorous as they illustrate gross incompetence, negligence and stupidity. I am also proud of Chrysler's many accomplishments, so some stories illustrate extreme competence on the part of some of those I associated with. Some of my associates at Chrysler worried I might write a book. Friends and relatives have mentioned I should write a book.

Books about the industry are numerous. Most are about the actions of top executives. This book is about day to day activities of a smarter than average engineer. In the other books they tell you that mistakes were made and then corrected. They never tell you about what these mistakes were. I do.

I am an unknown quantity outside of the circles I write about in the book. I suppose by now, most of them have forgotten about me. I was a Product Engineer A (grade 8) in the Chrysler structure. This is as high as you could get without actually supervising someone or becoming a spe-

1

cialist.

The book is non-fiction, the events are true. The rumors and stories I repeat are just that, rumors and stories I heard. Whether they are true or not, I can only guess, and sometimes support with other evidence. As discussion of certain persons will surely bring offense, the names have been changed to protect the privacy of the guilty and innocent. Their point of view is likely different, but not nearly as entertaining as mine. If any of you I write about notice your alias is in italics, it is because I thought you were an idiot! The few names I don't change are a few of my heroes and public figures.

For much of my 12 years at Chrysler, I had my dream job. My last three years were with Chrysler's advanced research group called "Liberty and Technical Affairs". I spent the first nine years primarily doing steering and suspension design work on Jeeps and Dodge trucks. I played a significant role in the redesign of the 1997 Jeep Wrangler. I still feel great pride whenever I see one on the road.

Jeeps are kind of a miracle too. Like cars that take us faster to places far beyond our mortal limits, Jeeps take us to places which are beyond the mortal limits of most humans; especially those who are overweight and out of shape like me. I live out West now. Out away from the population of our cities, are many beautiful places where one can experience the beauty of nature. Jeeps give access to this beauty that those of us who are not "granolas" would otherwise be denied. As a result, I have great affection for Jeeps.

Chrysler did a lot of things right in the 1990's primarily because of the great leadership of its president, Bob Lutz. I have often joked that I was the reason for their success; Chrysler had purchased AMC just to get me. However, I observe two major mistakes Chrysler made. The first was not handling its biggest investor properly, Kirk Kerkorian. The second was they had turned over their research to "Idiots." The first led to the merger with Daimler-Benz. This book is not about that. It is about the "Idiots."

I am saddened that Chrysler is now a subsidiary of a foreign corporation. The auto industry has shaped our society more than any other industry. Chrysler has been a major player. This book just debunks myths I held that the corporation needed smart people and was mostly comprised of such. Though I write about Chrysler, I assume similar antics are even more plentiful at larger corporations.

When I left, I took no documentation with me. This book is written from my memory, and public information. Chrysler is a fascinating company; I used to read everything I could about its history. Up until almost the end, I really enjoyed my career. People seem to be entertained when I tell them about my experiences at Chrysler.

In the book I introduce or reintroduce many "common sense" principles. Such as "if it ain't broke, don't fix it!" Some wise people have told me that "common sense" is not common, accordingly it is an oxymoron. I don't disagree as the book will illustrate. The general theme of the book is the havoc wreaked when "common sense" is ignored. I also share stories of success that resulted from the application of "common sense."

There are two kinds of chapters in the book -- chapters about people and chapters about technology. The people chapters are easier to read. If you are not technically inclined, it is possible the technical chapters will cure your insomnia.

Part 1

A NATURAL ENGINEER

Chapter 1

MY BACKGROUND

Smart people

I grew up in a home where we possessed an arrogance that we were smarter than everyone else. Both my parents were college educated, and my father was a successful architect. I have heard people talk about how it doesn't take a high IQ to be successful. It takes hard work and perseverance. With my superior intelligence, I have observed this to be true. I am personally an example. I'm very intelligent, yet considered a failure in most people's eyes.

When I left Chrysler, I was homeless and moved back in with my father. My oldest brother was living in a doublewide trailer. My other brother proudly sent a picture of the 14 foot wide trailer he purchased when he moved out of state. The three sons of a successful architect: one homeless and two living in manufactured housing. I find this very ironic. Not exactly an architect's dream for his children. Fortunately, my father can be proud of his daughter who married a dentist and lives in a large house.

Perhaps this book will be popular with those familiar with Dilbert. I'm not a fan myself, though I did buy Scott Adams' book <u>The Dilbert Principle</u> to specifically read the chapter about engineers. I considered myself one, and one of the best. Adams' description of engineers described me perfectly, with the exception of being a "trekkie". I 'm not a trekkie!

Laziness principle

One characteristic of engineers he didn't cover, perhaps because he is not one himself, is that of laziness. To the best of my knowledge, I am the original observer of this concept (I doubt it, but I'm the first to write about it because I'm too honest.) Honesty is an engineer characteristic according to Scott Adams. When Adam (of Adam and Eve fame) was kicked out of the garden and told he would eat by the sweat of his brow, he got tired of having to sweat so much to eat. He started inventing tools to make the job easier. And with that, the engineering profession began. It is a testament to the success of the early pioneers in the auto industry that the industry no longer values smart engineers. They invented themselves out of a job.

People commonly misunderstand the "laziness principle." I suppose because the word "lazy" is thought of in such a negative way. Here is a story from my life to illustrate the principle. At my father's architectural firm, one of the most unpleasant jobs was running blueprints. The smell of ammonia, paper cuts, handling big sheets of paper, and so forth, are not pleasant things. Most architects sent this work out to a print shop. Not my dad, he was smarter than that; he could get his kids to do it for half the cost. We got paid three cents a sheet, which, when we were fast, worked out to be about five dollars an hour. At the time he only paid his draftsmen about seven dollars an hour. It was good money back then. The majority of his business was designing church buildings. When the design was done, a set of blueprints and specifications was provided to each contractor (as many as 30) bidding on the construction of the building. There were only a few bids each year, so the opportunity to earn extra money by running blueprints only occurred occasionally. Because of the severe unpleasantness of the job (or because I was a lazy butt), I did whatever I could to get out of it. On one occasion, I was unable to wiggle out of it, or I needed the money or something. It was Monday; thirty sets of blueprints were due by Friday afternoon. My dad's staff offered to help after hours, as it seemed it would take a miracle to finish by Friday.

Monday, when I started running the prints, I found it frustratingly slow and boring. I got some duct tape and cardboard and started making some changes to the set up so it would be more automated. Some things I tried failed and others needed some refinement. By lunchtime, I had only completed one set, but I had the automation kinks worked out. An observer of my pace would conclude I would only have 10 sets done by Friday afternoon. My dad's staff was very nervous and overtures were made that I should abandon my attempts at automation, and "just do the job!" I assured them I'd get it done.

By Wednesday afternoon I had 30 sets completed -- two days early! I had made about nine dollars an hour. The motivation to automate came from my desire to get the nasty stuff done quickly, so I wouldn't have to do it very long. Some think I did this, so I would have time to do more unpleasant stuff to earn more money. Not so, it's like removing a Band-Aid; the faster you pull it off, the faster the pain is gone. It has to be removed some time, so why not make it as painless as possible. I have been called lazy by some in that I often go to extraordinary lengths to "minimize the pain." Hence, "the Laziness Principle."

A Natural

Before I tell the stories, I must establish my reputation as an engineer.

I don't remember, but they say I was taking stuff apart before I could walk. I remember wanting a doll house from Santa Claus when I was four years old. Not to play with dolls, but to put the house together; take it apart; put it together and so on. Later, I got a model train for Christmas and promptly disassembled it and couldn't put it back together. My parents had to return it to the hobby shop to be reassembled. My father had been a Navy aviator during WWII and often bought model planes for his sons. When I received money for my birthday or something, I usually bought a model car; never an airplane. Later, we were given Cox model airplanes with the little .049 engines. I promptly took them apart and imagined ways to put the engines in a model car.

In sixth grade, I was drawing pictures of cars, particularly the Ford Country Squire station wagon. I guess a sixth grader likes station wagons so he can get far away from his parents while riding in the car. The girl that sat in front of me in class used to act all impressed with my drawings. I wondered if she liked station wagons too. In seventh grade and beyond, she never said another word to me. I suppose in sixth grade it was cool, but in seventh grade, it was nerdy.

We lived in a relatively rural area of mesas and gullies in the foothills south of Salt Lake City. Opportunities to play in wide open areas with hills were abundant. When I was about 12, I had friends that were getting mini-bikes (lawnmower engine powered mini-motorcycles). I got a tired old used one for Christmas that year. (My mechanical genius uncle spent half a day fixing it before I could ride it). My older brother got a brand new welder that same year.

Near our home was a small airport where parachuting was popular. The airport had a dump in a small gully nearby. It was mostly filled with empty beer cans, some discarded airplane parts and occasionally an old airframe from a plane wreck. The mini-bike had died (it was mostly dead when I got it), but I learned to weld quite well with scrap metal salvaged from the airport dump. I bought a 10 hp Wisconsin industrial engine from a friend of my brother for $30. I figured this would be like supercharging my mini-bike. One problem; it wouldn't fit, so I used some old airplane tires and metal from the dump and created a tri-cart. I became somewhat infamous with the contraption among the neighbors. I would work on it for several hours after school, and then take it out for a test ride. I would get 50 feet from the house and it would break, so I would have to push it home. I did this everyday for two or three weeks until I finally gave up on it.

When I was about seven years old, my dad and older brothers built some kayaks with instructions from a do-it-yourself book. I had the opinion a real boat had an engine (you could only go so fast under human power, you know). When I was 13, I took that same book and built a mini-speed boat called the "Peanut." My dad went out and bought a 5 hp outboard for it, and I got my first speed boat. Now, with my boat building experience, my dad and brothers solicited my help in building a catamaran sailboat (why they insisted on a boat with no motor, I'll never know). The boat performed poorly, because they compromised on materials in too many areas making it too heavy. Despite the fact I preferred motorboats; I was a fairly skilled sailor and was qualified to make such a judgment of its performance.

The sail boat needed a trailer, I took some scrap metal, two big pipes and an old axle and made a trailer using my brother's welder. The pipes needed to have a bend put in them. Using the posts that held up our carport and my oldest brother's '62 Cadillac as a ballast, I designed a jig to put the bend in the pipes. I didn't even have a driver's license yet, but I had designed and built a roadworthy trailer. The trailer was later converted to haul snowmobiles and is still used today as a junk trailer.

Even before I had my driver's license, I had a reputation among friends and relatives for my ability to fix things. My cousin bought an old snowmobile for $24 at a church auction. It didn't run, so he called me. When there was snow on the ground, we would work on it all week long just to ride it for a few hours on Saturday until it broke down again. That was the beginning of my love of snowmobiling.

First cars

When I got my driver's license, my parents informed me that I couldn't own a car until I was 18. I was a "motor head;" I had three cars before I was 18. Technically I didn't "own" any of them (none were titled in my name). My brother gave me his '62 Cadillac, when my dad bought him a Vega. I inherited the Vega when my brother bought a '70 Dodge Challenger convertible. My brother wanted to sell his Challenger, and I was going to buy it. I wasn't yet 18, so my dad bought it, and I drove it my whole senior year in high school. It was in the top ten cool cars at my high school. In fact, when the Mercedes convertible that was to escort the homecoming royalty at halftime hadn't shown up, I was asked to drive the royalty around in the Challenger. Just three minutes before halftime the Mercedes arrived. So close to fame and yet so far, stupid Mercedes!

My dad always seemed to own a Plymouth, except when General Motors made a particularly awful car. We had not one, but two Vegas, and two Citations in our family. His affection for Chrysler was tied to his love of flying. He told me that Chryslers became his favorite car back when they introduced the Airflow model in the '30s. It had been designed to be aerodynamic just like airplanes were. When I was small, we had some Ramblers. We were Mormons; my dad had previously met George Romney who later was the president of American Motors and also a Mormon. Of course we had to have a Rambler, then back to Plymouths. After the two Citations, I converted dad to Toyotas. I think the Citation converted a lot of people to Japanese cars. When I started working at Chrysler, I converted him back to Chrysler products. I inherited my father's affection for the Chrysler brands. My friends and I affectionately called them "Mopars." In fact, when CB radios were big back in the 70's, my CB handle was the "Mopar Maniac."

Auto career

In high school, you are supposed to start deciding on a career. Race car driver! Richard Petty, AJ Foyt, and Don Garlits were my heroes. I began drag racing with the Challenger (cruising State Street in Salt Lake City). Later, I started going to the race track. I had bad luck and never much success. It was a thrill though. Now being much more mature and looking back, I realize I didn't lack skill; I just didn't have any support. The great drivers had parents and large extended families that supported them. I always went to the racetrack alone. My lack of success didn't discourage me from pursuing this dream; I just figured I needed more experience and money.

My mother often told me I was college material. College was not in my plans. How could school help me win any races? A high school friend, Ken Davis, who knew about my love for cars, told me about the Automotive Engineering Technology program at Weber State College in Ogden, Utah. I wasn't interested in college at the time, but my mother convinced me to take the ACT test anyway. I had my results sent to Weber State.

The summer between my sophomore and junior year in high school, I got a job at the local country club. I worked in the pro shop. My duties were retrieving and storing the member's golf clubs, picking up the golf balls on the driving range and maintaining the electric golf carts. Working on the electric golf carts was my first job as a mechanic. I got pretty good at it. When I resigned in the fall, my boss tried to talk me into staying just to be their cart mechanic. I declined. I really didn't like the guy very much.

Before graduation from high school, I got a job at a tire market. I figured it was my first step in becoming an auto mechanic, which would help me in my ultimate goal of winning the Indy 500. I learned a lot about tires; from semi-truck tires on down. The auto service industry has a lot of dishonesty and shady practices. This was my first exposure to it. The owner

9

often sold work to customers whose cars didn't need the work and pressured me to do the same. I only lasted two months. I quit after we had an argument about a customer I thought he was ripping off.

Three days later, I started at the Sears Auto Center. They let me go two weeks later after I was blamed for failing to put oil in a customer's car. Actually, one of the managers moved the car before I was finished with it, and I forgot about it. I would have noticed there was no oil in the car, if I had moved it. I learned to never let anyone move a car I was working on.

Within a week, I got a job at another tire store. They were over staffed and two weeks later they laid me off. I wasn't having much success at becoming a mechanic and I hit rock bottom. I worked the next few weeks for a temporary labor service, sweeping broken glass, moving office furniture, etc. At the temporary labor place, I had the privilege to hang out with bums and hear their incredible stories of fortune. One guy told us about a car he bought somewhere for $50 and drove to St. Louis, where he sold it for $75. He was in the big money.

I answered an ad for an apprentice auto mechanic. The pay was not very good, but I was promised I would learn a lot. It was a small independent shop with the owner's wife keeping the books, the owner as a mechanic, a second mechanic and me. My boss, Ron Baker, did teach me a lot, and he was more honest than anyone else I've ever met in the industry. I learned some tricks and built an engine for my Challenger. I started to have some success at the race track. In fact, my confidence level grew until I was ready to race in a weekend event. If I have a weakness, it is my lack of attention to detail. I failed to check that all the nuts and bolts were tight. The air cleaner stud came loose and got sucked inside the engine. Antifreeze was dripping from the cracked block onto the track. Needless to say, I towed the car home.

After a year as an apprentice, I started getting bored with being a mechanic. I had learned to do everything my boss did, though he wouldn't let me do alignments except on my own car. Ironically, alignment became my specialty at Chrysler. Often while performing repairs, I noticed how some design changes could be made to improve the cars or make them easier to service. This got me thinking a career designing cars would be more interesting than just fixing them. I resigned from the apprentice job and headed to Ogden to go to college at Weber State. Ron told me he was glad and sad to see me go, "I'll miss your help, but you can't reach your potential here." An Automotive Engineering Technology program sounded like just the ticket.

During college, I worked part time as a mechanic at another Sears Auto Center. Sears is a good place to buy car batteries, but a significant number of customers that came in with low batteries didn't need a new battery. Most often it was just a loose alternator belt (excellent training by Ron Baker), so I tightened the belt and sent the customers on their way. The management pressured me to sell a battery in these situations. They also accused me of being "lazy." I had a very easy going attitude and walked slower than the other help. I was steady and rarely took breaks. Sears kept track of our productivity, and though I was only part-time, my productivity was better than most full-time mechanics (when customers noticed my honesty, I could sell them the work their cars truly did need). My productivity numbers didn't matter to the Sears management; they wanted me to "look" busier! They cut my hours and put me on call. I picked up my tools a few days later, and that was that.

Chapter 2

WHY CAN'T I FIND A GOOD MECHANIC?

Excellent mechanic

I was an excellent mechanic, but other than Ron Baker, I have rarely met other good/honest mechanics. When people learn that I was a mechanic, they ask me "Where can I find a good/honest mechanic?" I used to refer them to Ron, but he has since retired. I now tell those who inquire, "good mechanics are rare." If an individual possesses the intelligence to be a good mechanic, he or she will get into a career that pays better. I did.

I suppose if a mechanic is reading this, he might be offended. I am not too worried, most mechanics are illiterate. Oops, another insult. Well, if a mechanic is reading this, there is a good chance he is a good one. You see, no one can know everything needed to be a good mechanic, cars are too complicated. So a good mechanic will read a service manual.

Illiterate mechanic

My first encounter with illiterate adults came during college while working at another auto repair shop. Ron Baker had taught me most automatic transmission problems could be solved by simply servicing the transmission. Back then that involved changing the filter and fluid, and adjusting the settings on things called "bands."

This shop was a family business. I was the only one that wasn't family. Grandpa rebuilt carburetors, even when they didn't need it. The oldest son managed the place and occasionally worked on cars. The younger son who was still twice my age was a mechanic and also their snowmobile mechanic (they were also a small snowmobile dealership). The grandson, a little older than me was also a mechanic.

The grandson had a motor home that was having some transmission problems. He was going to have the transmission rebuilt. They didn't rebuild transmissions at their establishment, so this would be quite costly. I overheard him telling the symptoms to his dad, and his dad agreed it would need to be rebuilt soon. I interrupted and asked if they had tried servicing it yet. They had not. I then suggested that servicing the transmission might correct the problems and it could save them a lot of money. They had never serviced a transmission before. They weren't totally convinced, I was just a young college kid, after all. Nevertheless, they let me at it.

I pulled the pan and drained the fluid out of the transmission. I walked over to where they kept the service manuals and grabbed the appropriate one to look up the specification for the band settings. I took it back to where the motor home was and opened it. The pages stuck together like it had never been opened before. They rushed over and put a halt to my work. "Why are you looking in a manual, don't you know what you are doing?" they accused. "I need to look up the specification, because there are different specifications on different models. I don't memorize them all, you know." I answered, not realizing what I was dealing with. It took me a half an hour to convince them I did know what I was doing. They finally relented and let me finish. It cured all the symptoms with the transmission and they were duly impressed.

Even from this experience, it still did not occur to me that some of them were illiterate. They received a batch of new snowmobiles. They were the first Polaris models with the "Indy" suspension. The suspension needed to be assembled when the machine was removed from the crate. The younger son approached me and handed me the instructions for doing this and asked, "What does this mean to you?" pointing at some text below a picture. It seemed clear to me, so I responded, "Just what it says." and handed the paper back to him. He then admitted to me that he could not read. This just blew my mind; a middle aged adult that could not read!

Personal experiences

Because of the "Laziness" principle, I have often tried unsuccessfully to find competent mechanics to repair things. In the end, I buy a service manual and do it myself. This is much easier than finding a competent mechanic. In fact, now when I buy a new toy (snowmobile or PWC), I just order the service manual first thing. For some reason, I always get the lemons, and they need a lot of work. So to enjoy these things right away, I need to be able to fix them. I experience "Murphy's Law" more than anyone else I have ever met. When I was a teenager, I was too poor to ever pay a mechanic to fix my stuff. So for a time I assumed there were competent mechanics like me. I tried on several occasions to get things fixed by taking them to mechanics.

While in college, my dad purchased a speed boat. Finally my family got it; a real boat has an engine. I became a very avid water-skier. The boat had an old 115 hp Evinrude outboard motor. My boating buddies dubbed me "Evanrude." The first summer we had the boat, the engine had some problems. I figured, since my dad would pay for it, rather than fix it myself, I'd take it to a boat mechanic. I didn't know what was wrong anyway. We got it back from the mechanic and it acted exactly the same. I bought a service manual, and fixed it myself.

I had an on and off again girlfriend in college whose family had a boat. One day we went waterskiing in their boat. We got to the lake and it wouldn't start. I looked at it and got it running. I wasn't sure how long it would run. Not long as it happened. I wondered if anyone would be able to fix it besides me. Shortly thereafter, we broke-up. A mutual friend informed me the boat spent the whole summer in the shop and was never fixed. In fact, they gave up on the old gal and bought a new boat.

I love technology, so when I bought myself a brand new snowmobile, I got one with electronic fuel injection (EFI). Shortly thereafter, I was riding it on thin ice; it broke through into 20 feet of water. I lived through the experience and the snowmobile was retrieved just a few hours later. The local dealer's eyes bugged out at the thought of billing my insurance company for all the repairs.

Just the year before, I had totaled a snowmobile. I was afraid another big claim would make me uninsurable. I declined to have this dealer make the repairs. I figured I could do it myself, probably for less than the deductible anyway.

In my conversations with this dealer, he seemed pretty unscrupulous. When I picked up the snowmobile, I noticed some spare parts were missing off of it. I asked for the parts and was told they were out of stock and had used mine for an emergency on the trail. They had the identical model as mine on the showroom floor. I told them they would give me the parts off of that one or I would call the police. Suddenly, they were no longer out of the parts.

The EFI module didn't like the water. I replaced it and repaired everything else. I had purchased a service manual. There were some calibration adjustments that still needed to be made to get it to run properly. I didn't have the tools to make these adjustments. I took it to my dealer near my home and asked if they would do this. They didn't know how, and wouldn't admit it. After the sled was at this dealer a week, they told me I needed to replace more parts. I lost my cool and called them idiots. I then ordered the tools to do it myself. One hour after I got home with the tools, I had it running right. Their mechanic probably couldn't read either.

My sister has a personal watercraft that got swamped. She took it to a mechanic in Page, Arizona. The mechanic said the crankshaft was bent and the engine needed to be replaced. With the new engine, it still would not run properly. She took it back and was told the carburetors needed to be overhauled. She asked why this was not done when the engine was replaced. She paid for the carburetor overhaul and it still ran poorly. She had invested $3500 in repairs on the thing and it ran no better than when they started. In fact they paid less for another used PWC. She took it to a different mechanic in Flagstaff. They said they didn't think the carburetors had been rebuilt. She started legal action against the shop in Page. She brought the PWC to me with the carburetors in bags. I put them together, and took it to a lake. It took me about 3 hours of tinkering with the carburetors to get it to run properly. Now it goes like stink.

Finding a mechanic

I don't know where you can find a good mechanic. Unless you are related to me, you ain't gonna find one! From my experiences and observations, I have some ideas that may help you locate one. Because I do all my own work, these methods are not proven!

Look at the shop's service manuals. If a few are laying out with greasy finger prints on the pages, maybe somebody there can read. That is a big plus.

Dealing with Dealers

Often dealers will have one or two decent mechanics. However, you will pay through the nose. This may be worth it, if your problem actually gets fixed. Dealers have access to the factory knowledge. However, having worked in a dealership, the factory's policies nearly always invite dishonesty.

New car dealers pay their mechanics with a system which is called "flat rate." This means a mechanic is paid the same amount for the same job, no matter how long he takes to get it done. An example is repairing a head gasket on a 4-cylinder engine. There is a time guide book that specifies the job to take 5 hours. The mechanic is paid $20/hour, so is paid $100 to do this job. The customer is charged $65/hour, thus paying $325 labor for the job. A mechanic who specializes in the job can get it done in about 3 hours; therefore making $33/hour. I have no problem with this method of compensation for the work; however, this is not how it happens at a new car dealer.

The auto manufacturer knows that a specialist can do the job in 3 hours, therefore when the job is done under warranty; the mechanic is only paid 3 hours time or $60 for the job. Because of the high quality of the car, the mechanic will only do the job occasionally, so he will be a bit slower (he has to take time to read the service manual) than a specialist, and will complete the job in 5 hours. Then he will only be making $12/hour. This does not make for a happy mechanic! It is rare that a mechanic will finish warranty work in the time allotted.

To placate the mechanics, dealers allow them to "bid" (more accurately, jack up the price) on non-warranty repair. On a non-warranty head gasket job, the mechanic will offer to do it for 8 hours of labor charges or $520. The service writer will call the customer and through intimidating sales tactics, get the customer to authorize the repair at the inflated price. You will pay through the nose to get it repaired at the dealer. The manufacturer pays the mechanic $60 for a $100 job. The customer pays the mechanic $160 for the same $100 job. Therefore, the warranty work is essentially subsidized by paying customers. I suppose if it gets fixed, it may be worth it to you. The warranty work is typically given to an inexperienced mechanic. The dealer wants to keep their good mechanics happy. Warranty work doesn't make them happy. Dealers can be a possible place to find a good mechanic, but expect to pay a lot more. You will be subsidizing the factory's warranty work.

While employed at Chrysler, I leased company cars. All service to these vehicles was done at the company's expense. We were supposed to take the vehicle to any local dealer for service and repair. However, even in this circumstance I found dealing with a dealer so unpleasant, I would usually get the parts on my own accord and make the repairs myself (I was driving Chryslers, new Chryslers need repairs!). When I worked as a mechanic at a Dodge dealer, there was one other mechanic who was very competent. Dealing with a dealer is a hassle, occasionally it may be worth it.

Barry Manilow test

Another clue; can the mechanic stand to listen to Barry Manilow? Even when songs were played on the radio that I didn't care for, I usually didn't bother to change the station. However, when I heard Barry's voice, it was particularly irritating, and I always changed the station. It sounded so "fake" to me. I also tried the word "dishonest" to explain the irritation to others. Ron Baker who favored "soft rock" more than me, was also irritated by Barry. The radio in Ron's shop would usually be tuned to a soft rock radio station which frequently played Barry. When Ron was in a good mood, he'd just yell "turn that damn thing off!" when a Manilow song came on. When he was in a bad mood, you learned to duck as soon as you heard Barry's voice. A wrench would be flung at the radio without any warning. We never kept nice radios at the shop; because they were frequently replaced.

Ron was one of the most honest men I ever met. I am also an honest man. Honest men are irritated by the "dishonest" sound of Barry Manilow's voice. If your mechanic turns down the radio or changes stations when a

Barry song comes on, he is an honest mechanic!

Toolbox test

This might be another method for spotting a good mechanic, but should be combined with the shop manual test for literacy. A look at a mechanics toolbox can be a good indicator of the mechanics competence.

If the toolbox is brand new, spotless and exceptionally large, stay away! If his toolbox is old, with several smaller add on boxes; he has potential. A good mechanic does not feel a need to impress anyone with the look of his toolbox. His work is sufficient. An incompetent mechanic feels the need to make an impression and always has the latest and largest toolbox. At Chrysler's labs and at a dealership, I've met a few mechanics that were nearly as competent as Ron Baker; all had the smallest and oldest toolboxes in their respective shops. Ron's toolbox was really old too. I've shared this indicator, and I always get an argument. Still, they keep asking, "Why can't I find a good mechanic?"

Chapter 3

FORMAL TRAINING

A quiet student

In my seventh grade history class, I wanted to be popular; so I would read the textbook and cheerfully raise my hand to answer the teacher's questions. As you might realize, this didn't enhance my popularity. Being the smart guy I was, by the eighth grade, I never volunteered to answer questions in class. The ridicule stopped, and I no longer had to sit by myself at lunch. I usually got good grades with the exception of my senior year in high school, but rarely could a teacher remember my name. Weber State was no different. I never volunteered a word to anyone, teacher or student. I pulled good grades, but pretty much kept to myself and didn't pay much attention to anyone. One day I was eating lunch with some other students who were discussing how difficult a particular class had been. They mentioned only one student had received an A. I had received an A. It occurred to me then, I was doing better than my fellow students.

Some instructors noticed me, but others didn't. One day while studying in the department lounge outside the faculty offices, I overheard the department head, Ross Eskelson and another faculty member talking. Mr. Eskelson pointed at a name on a sheet of paper, "Do you know who this is? I've had him in two classes and given him A's, and I don't have a clue who he is." The other faculty member said, "He's right there." and pointed at me. From that time on, it seemed Eskelson (as we called him) became my mentor. Mr. Eskelson took a strong interest in me and never allowed me to be silent in class again.

Ross Eskelson had retired early from industry and taught school to keep himself busy. Earlier in his life, he started a company that manufactured tracked vehicles which were used primarily for grooming ski slopes. Mr. Eskelson often told us stories about the design of these vehicles to illustrate engineering principles. He often spewed out principles as axioms which I have often quoted to colleagues over the years.

Eskelson principle #1

"It's not what you don't know that gets you in trouble; it's what you know that ain't so!" To me this statement was self explanatory, but whenever I repeat it, it seems I have to tell a story: When I was about 6 years old, I was sleeping in a bunk bed in our partially finished basement bedroom. Only one piece of sheetrock had been installed on the ceiling directly above the bed. I was sleeping on the top bunk and woke up to go to the bathroom. In the dark, the one piece of sheet rock looked like the top bunk and I "knew" I was on the lower bunk. I leapt onto the floor several feet below and broke my foot. What I "knew" wasn't so! The principle also has application in engineering and many other aspects of life.

Eskelson principle #2

This can also be called the "career placement" principle. "The top students go on to work for the top companies. The average students go to work for the companies that supply the top companies. The students, who just barely survive the program, go on to work for the government and make the rules for the rest of us." I have observed this to be true in almost all professions (an exception would be law enforcement).

The principle fails to account for those, who upon graduation can't even get a job with the government. So, I have added to the principle; those that cannot even get a job with the government, go on to graduate school and get a Masters degree and become our bosses. Some, even with Masters Degrees, are still so incompetent they cannot find a job. They go on to get a PhD and become instructors or "special scientists" at large corporations or the government. I've never had a boss with a PhD, but have worked with a few "special scientists."

Many of you with advanced degrees will be offended by this, which is good. It means that you have understood the concept and are intelligent. I have some hope for you. Some professions, such as medical doctor, require a Doctorate to even practice. In this case, the theory does not apply. Generally to practice engineering, only a BS degree is required, so an engineer with a PhD is an idiot! In my 12 years at Chrysler, I observed no exceptions to this rule. However, I did receive some good advice from a PhD "idiot" once. Perhaps it was to justify his lack of productivity? Here it is; "Solving difficult engineering problems is like putting together a large picture puzzle. Even though pieces are being put in place, progress is not visible. Eventually, as the pieces get put in place, the picture will appear, so don't get discouraged." I've used this advice to keep myself encouraged when tackling huge problems in my life. Incidentally, I never saw this particular PhD put even one piece of the puzzle together in the three years I worked with him.

Changing light bulbs

I know this is harsh for those of you with Masters and PhDs. To illustrate a typical experience with those having advanced degrees, I'll pick on a former roommate and tell the light bulb story. About the time AMC merged with Chrysler, I had a roommate who had a degree in finance and an MBA. He was a new hire to Chrysler. His salary was about $10k a year more than mine, because he had the MBA. This irritated me.

One morning as I was on my way out the door, he informed me the bathroom light bulb had burned out. I told him there were light bulbs on the shelf in the closet and left. When I got home, it appeared the new light bulb had already burned out. I changed the bulb. When my MBA roommate got home, I mentioned to him the light bulb he changed had already burned out. He then said he never changed it, he didn't know how. My jaw hit the floor.

As you can imagine, this peaked my curiosity. How does a man get through graduate school no less, and not know how to change a light bulb? His answer was, "My dad always changed them while I was growing up. Since then, I've always had roommates who've done it." "Didn't you ever watch your dad change one?" I probed further, "It's not hard. Weren't you a little curious to learn to do something your dad did?" I showed him how, however I doubt he has changed one since. I know mentally challenged people that routinely handle this task. Just like the illiterate mechanic, I just could not comprehend an adult male not knowing how to change a light bulb!

Wrong track

Contrary to my belief and reason for attending Weber State, the Automotive Engineering Technology Department did not prepare students for careers as design engineers. Graduates went on to be service representatives for auto and truck companies and the like. Nobody told me this. After I was more than two years into the program, I figured it out. A design engineer from GM had come to speak to us. I was sure this was what I wanted to do. A design engineer required a Bachelor of Science in Mechanical Engineering. A Bachelor of Science in Automotive Engineering Technology was not equivalent. A BSME required a big dose of calculus. (It is interesting to note that it was rare to meet somebody with a BSME that remembered anything about calculus.) The BSAET substituted automotive systems classes for the higher math.

I counseled with several of my professors and came up with two options: First, I could transfer to another school which offered a BSME. The

AET program at Weber was not accredited; very few of my credits would transfer. I would essentially be starting over, and it would take four more years to get the BSME. Second, I could finish at Weber with a BSAET, and then pursue a Masters degree in mechanical engineering. This would also take four years to accomplish. I would then have two degrees and be qualified to be a boss. I didn't know about the boss part then, as I had not yet modified Eskelson principle #2. I decided the second option was the best, and I continued at Weber State.

SAE Mini-Baja

One of the requirements for graduation was a senior class project. The Society of Automotive Engineers (SAE) sponsors several collegiate student design competitions each year. The class the year before had entered the Southwest SAE Mini-Baja competition and had finished quite respectably, in the middle of the pack. My senior class chose to do the same thing. The project was fun. We selected a project manager from our group (not me, I was still quiet), and each student was given responsibilities for the design of the vehicle. My assignment was the steering and suspension including alignment. A Mini-Baja vehicle is a miniature dune buggy powered by an 8 hp Briggs and Stratton engine. A full roll-cage was required, and no engine modifications were allowed.

Our group was not particularly talented. After all, who goes to a college that doesn't have an accredited program? Not much progress was being made on the project, and Eskelson was not very happy. He mentioned that with the previous class, he had held their hands to get them through the project. He wasn't going to do the same for us. If we didn't get it done, we wouldn't graduate. He didn't believe we could do it. Well this lit a fire under me, and I informally took over as project manager. I did most of the design work, and almost all of the fabrication of the car.

Eskelson principle #3

"Don't reinvent the wheel. Don't be too proud to steal another's idea, it is a lot less trouble." This is a fairly widely known principle that did not originate from Eskelson. He repeated it often enough that I give him credit here.

Eskelson had taken many photographs of the competition's mini-baja cars the previous year. The car we took to the competition looked very similar to the first place car from the year before. I found in my own career this was where my real talent was; I was good at taking someone else's idea and getting it to work. I had the ability to analyze someone else's design and to improve upon it. Rarely did I originate an idea. The common saying, "imitation is the sincerest form of flattery," has application in this principle. Eskelson said, "swallow your pride, flatter them and win." As in the case of the Chrysler minivan, Ford and GM refused to copy it (they were not about to flatter Mr. Iacocca with imitation!) and failed to make an impact on that market. Years later, they did copy Chrysler and had successful minivans of their own.

The mini-baja competition was to take place about two weeks after our spring break. We had a lot of fabrication and testing to do, so we didn't take a spring break. Weber had an outstanding machine shop lab with about 30 lathes and numerous milling machines. The welding lab was equally well equipped. I learned to weld when I was young, and learned to use machines in high school. The problem was, these labs were not our department's, and we weren't allowed to use the equipment, except during certain hours. The hours were insufficient for us to get the project done on time. We figured out how to break into the shops and were careful to leave no messes. During spring break we got a lot done. When spring break ended, it was a little harder, because we had to wait until everybody left the shops, before we could break in.

For several weeks before the competition, I'd leave my apartment at 7: 00 a.m. and work on the mini-baja car until I had a class. Between and after classes I was back working on it. I didn't usually return home until 10:00 or 11:00 p.m. I imagine this is what racing is like, I'm glad I didn't pursue it as a career. We placed third overall in the competition. Not bad, considering most of the competing cars were actually creations of some experienced professor. We were elated!

Replacing Lido

The experience with the mini-baja dramatically increased my confidence. I was interviewed by the local news, received some scholarship money and received much praise from the Weber State faculty. More than one professor expressed I was a natural at engineering, and they expected great things in my future. One professor expressed I should start my career right now, before graduation. Others said I didn't need to obtain a Master's degree. Though I did forego the Master's, I continued and graduated from Weber. I figured I was ready to head to Detroit and replace Lido (a popular nickname for Lee Iacocca) as the head of Chrysler.

Chapter 4

FOOT IN THE DOOR

Looking for a job

My first choice of employers was Chrysler. At the time, Chrysler had an aftermarket performance parts division called "DirectConnection"; I thought this would be the best place for me. I got a response to the résumé I sent to DirectConnection, recommending I gain some experience first. It recommended that experience with Chrysler was preferred. Engineers with Chrysler typically had responsibility for more parts than an engineer with GM or Ford.

Six months after graduation from Weber, I had interviewed with several automotive related companies, nevertheless I hadn't received any job offers. Things weren't looking good. I decided if I wanted to get a job with a car company, I needed to be on their doorstep when they had an opening. I packed up enough stuff to fill my little Toyota truck and headed to Detroit (note the freedom to pack my stuff and go where I wanted).

After six weeks in Detroit and no job, I was about to give up. Then just before Christmas 1985, I landed a position with GM. I didn't actually work for the General. I was a "contract engineer" employed on a GM contract by Technical Services Inc (TSI). This is a very common practice in the industry. When the work load is heavy, you bring in contract employees and pay them a premium (often better than direct employees). When the work slows down, you let them go. It is very difficult to fire or lay off a direct employee as I later learned. Hiring contractors was also a way for a manager to have more employees, without first getting permission from the corporate personnel department. In large corporations, a manager's importance is often defined by how many people are under him/her. Managers at GM hired many contract employees to expand their staff when they could, so they could expand their importance. This seemed to be the reason I was hired, just to help my manager build his little empire.

I had a job, but little or no work to do. I designed a small L-shaped bracket for an electric antenna and learned what a CHMSL (center high mounted stop lamp) is, in the six-months I worked there. I now understood why cars cost so much; they had to pay for a bunch of people to sit around on their derrières. The rest of the time, I read trade journals, slept in the men's room or went shopping; coming back just in time to punch out. This filled my 53 hour work week. I was bored and not sure this was what I wanted.

It's even hard to lay-off contract employees: so what they did was cut us all down to 44 hours a week. Most needed the 53 hours just to pay their bills. About 80 percent of the contract employees found other jobs with overtime. They were gone in a week. Observing this, I determined I never wanted to be dependent on overtime to pay my bills. From that point on, I avoided working overtime as much as I could. This was not a career enhancing choice, but one I never regretted.

Working with no skill

As I mentioned, there was very little work for me to do in the six months I worked at GM for TSI. I wasn't necessarily hired for my skills either. It was fairly common at the time for someone with no skills to get hired with a fraudulent résumé because many understood the concept of empire building and were glad to oblige. If the individual was sharp enough, once hired, he could get someone who was competent and bored out of their mind to do the little amount of work he did get assigned. He collected a paycheck for several months or years before it would be discovered he had no skills. In time, some would develop a few skills. I met individuals on several occasions that fit both of these categories. After they had collected paychecks for months or years, the résumés were no longer fraudulent. This was one method idiots used to proliferate in the auto industry.

Direct hire

Even though it was a cut in pay, contract engineers generally desired to be hired directly with one of the automakers. That way you were set for life. They would never fire you and you got great benefits. In my job search before the grand position at TSI, I had sent a résumé to American Motors Corporation. AMC lost money every year but somehow stayed in business. In March 1986, I received a call and subsequently had two interviews. I expected an offer from them, but the weeks turned into months, and I decided that the 44 hours a week at TSI was fine. Early in June, I got an offer with a substantial pay increase. I accepted the offer and on June 23, 1986, started as an Engineer in Training (EIT) at American Motors Corporation. A direct hire with no cut in pay!

My manager at GM discouraged me from taking the position, because security with American Motors was very questionable in his mind. I ignored him and took the job anyway. In retrospect, since a BS in Mechanical

Engineering was required to be a direct hire at Chrysler, Ford, or General Motors; this was my only opportunity to be a direct hire engineer with my "lesser" degree. Application of Eskelson's principle #2, "the career placement principle," prevented me from becoming a direct hire at the larger companies, because I didn't even have the minimum required degree. With the constant forecasts of doom and gloom for American Motors, they were not as selective in their desperation to staff their departments adequately, and I was able to get a job there. AMC was my foot in the door at Chrysler. I still remember the days at AMC with much fondness. It was a fun place to work. Even though I only worked at AMC for a year before merging with Chrysler, I always thought of myself as an AMC employee. AMC created in me attitudes that I never relinquished.

On more than one occasion, primarily because of my religion, I met and had brief conversations with George Romney, the former president of AMC. He always said they should have stuck with the Rambler, and they would have been successful. I can't say I agree, but at the time they had Jeep and that seemed to keep them afloat. The French automaker, Renault, was the current owner of AMC. The Renault Alliance (insiders called it the "appliance") was not selling well, despite being Motor Trend's "Car of the Year." Motor Trend destroyed the stature of the award with the selection of the Alliance, by the way. Recently, when the Mitsubishi spokesman disclosed in a commercial that car companies win awards because they buy off the press, he wasn't kidding. I digress here; back to the story.

A Frenchman, Francois Castaing, was the current Engineering Vice President, or my boss's, boss's, boss's boss. He held what he called "breakfast meetings" with all the recent new hires, where we could ask him questions. I asked him why the Appliance (I said "Alliance") was not selling well, when the Japanese were doing so well with small cars. He replied in typical French arrogance, "It's a good car, but Americans are stupid." I may have taken some literary license here, but that was the message I got from his response.

Mr. Castaing held these breakfast meetings on a regular basis, so he would stay in touch with the "troops." It is partly because such efforts were made by American Motors management, that it was such a fun place to work. Everyone had access to Castaing and knew where his office was. The openness ended when Chrysler took over.

The "Appliance" was not entirely a derogatory moniker. The AMC engineering center, on Plymouth Road in Detroit had once been a Nash Kelvinator factory where refrigerators were manufactured. AMC was the product of the merger of Hudson and Nash; thus, "Appliance" was also a term with reference to the history of the building. The AMC 2.5 liter engine held onto the heritage too and was referred to as a "Nash" motor.

Designing cars

The process of designing a car involves many departments. The idea for a new vehicle or the renewal of an existing vehicle is first formed in the Program Management department. This department does customer research and tries to determine what features and options new cars should have. They never do any design work, so we thought of their staff as inferior when in fact, they are the most influential.

The preliminary design work is then done by the Advanced Vehicle Packaging (AVP) group where feasibility is determined. Often, programs are cancelled at this stage because of feasibility, marketing or political reasons.

Once the decision to go forward with a program is made, the design is given to the Design departments. The different systems in a car such as the engine, transmission, body and chassis, etc. are divided among several design departments. These departments design the parts and select the suppliers that will build the parts, and also ensure the parts are manufactured and delivered to the assembly plants.

The Vehicle Development department builds and tests the prototype vehicles to ensure the vehicles work and perform to the desired goals (determined by Program Management). Part of the Vehicle Development department is the Vehicle Dynamics department. This group does the fine tuning of the vehicle's ride and handling characteristics, which involves selecting spring rates and tuning shock absorbers.

The Manufacturing Engineering department gets to figure out how to put all the parts together after they have been designed. The entire process takes anywhere from five to seven years. Some manufacturers have bragged they have done it in just one to two years, but the time they quote is only the time from program approval; when AVP gives the design to the Design departments. It doesn't include the advanced work where feasibility is being determined.

Engineer in Training

The "Engineer in Training" program was scheduled for 18 months and consisted of three rotations in different departments. My first rotation was in the Vehicle Development department. I was responsible for the maintenance of the "problem log" database for what eventually became the Eagle Premier. Development engineers would drive the prototype cars and discover problems that needed to be resolved, and then I would enter them into the database. These entries became part of a report that was published about every two weeks. The report tracked the problems and corrective actions. When I arrived, the report took three days to print out because of some gross inefficiencies in how the database was programmed. Six months later, after I had fiddled with the program, you could print a copy of the entire report in about an hour. Once in a while I got to drive a car, but mostly, I helped the secretaries with the database.

My manager at the time was Jean Claude Revel; his boss was Regis Valet: two Frenchmen (with aliases). Valet had personally written the code for the "problem log". On numerous occasions he had ordered me not to change the database, telling me to, "just do the job!" in his thick French accent. (I'd heard that before). As "lazy" as I was, I ignored Regis and continued to refine and improve the database until my assignment was up. Because I always delivered the reports accurately and on time, Valet did little to punish my insubordination.

My next assignment was with the Engine Design department. Basically I remember three projects there: 1) I tried to use a computer to simulate air flow in an intake manifold (unsuccessfully); 2) I adapted a supercharger to the AMC 2.5 liter engine ("Nash" motor); and 3) I did preliminary designs for an MPI (multi point injection) intake manifold for the same engine.

To adapt a supercharger to an engine, usually the compression ratio of the engine must be lowered. I had very little budget to work with, but I forged some relationships with the right people (American Motors people always tried to help each other out) and was able to obtain parts to lower the compression ratio. The "Nash" motor, at the time, was a throttle body fuel-injected engine. For the supercharger project, it was desirable to make it into a multi-point fuel injection (MPI) engine. I did get the engine built with the supercharger on it and ready for testing in a dynamometer cell, but it never got tested because other projects always had higher priority. Nevertheless, it was a fun experience.

AMC products

The bright spot at AMC was the compact Jeep Cherokee. In my opinion, the success of the Cherokee is why Chrysler bought AMC. Introduced in 1984, it was a hit, because it was the only 4-door compact SUV on the market. It was a money maker for AMC. In 1987, the 4.0 liter in-line six cylinder engine replaced the Chevy 2.8 liter V6 as the premium engine for the Cherokee. The new engine was rated at 170 hp vs. the 125 hp of the V6. It suddenly was a high performance vehicle to boot, and AMC couldn't build them fast enough.

Putting the 4.0 liter in the Cherokee was no small feat. The story I was told was the executive in charge of the design of the Cherokee hated the

AMC inline 6 cylinder engine (the 4.2 liter) and specifically designed the Cherokee so it would not fit. The Nash 2.5 liter engine was fitted with fuel injection and the General Motors 2.8 liter V6 with oil leaks were the original engine options for the Cherokee.

The Comanche pick-up truck shared the Assembly line with the Cherokee. It was not as profitable as the Cherokee. We lost money on every "Appliance" we built. In a Town Hall meeting of all AMC employees, an executive joked, "The bad news is; Alliance and Comanche sales are down. The good news is; Alliance and Comanche sales are down." We were losing less money because we were selling fewer Alliances. Building fewer Comanches allowed us to build more of the more profitable Cherokees.

There was a last attempt to breathe life back into the Renault Alliance with a "pocket rocket" version. Unfortunately for the Alliance, the Cherokee with the 4.0 liter engine would out accelerate it. The press didn't let this fact go unnoticed. Sales did not improve for the Alliance.

Part 2

A REAL ENGINEER

Chapter 5

PROBLEM SOLVER

First engineering position

Chrysler had purchased AMC, and there was a flood of employees leaving. Most of the French left with one notable exception, Castaing. Chrysler put a hiring freeze in place shortly after the merger, and fleeing employees could not be replaced. We were initially told we would complete the final rotation of the EIT program, but a few weeks later, the four remaining trainees (many EITs left too) were given a list of six critical positions that needed to be filled. We were the only ones available to fill them. I selected the position in the Steering and Suspension design group, and my training was over. The manager, Tom Steel, said I didn't have the experience he desired; however since no one else was available, he'd take me. I was not fond of Mr. Steel either, but the other positions were not as interesting. There was not a choice in the engine group, which I would have preferred.

Tom assigned me to work with "Roger *Dimwit*" (note the italics), known as "The Flame" because of his flaming red hair and flaming incompetence as an engineer. Roger had deluded himself into thinking he was an extremely competent engineer. In the desperate AMC environment (at least I thought this the reason); some flaming idiots were brought on board. Roger's assignment was the steering column and related parts. I was assigned to assist him.

The first assignment he gave me was to coordinate building a test fixture to measure steering wheel feel (it actually measured friction; you can't really measure "feel"). This was ridiculous, and everyone knew it. How do you explain this to someone who is delusional? Everyone would just nod their heads when Roger explained it, and laughed at him when he left. They pitied me for being assigned to work with him. I recognized the stupidity of the assignment, and with only one stupid project to do, I was back to biding my time. I read trade journals and books in our Technical Library hoping for something to change. Change came quickly. Mr. Steel transferred, and "The Flame" was laid off. I didn't report to anybody for a few weeks.

Former AMC employees had to interview with Chrysler, and most, like me, were offered their present jobs. If you were not offered your present job, you could interview for positions in other departments. "The Flame" interviewed a lot, but never received an offer; and was eventually laid off. I felt kind of sorry for him. A short time later, after a meeting, I was in the restroom, standing next to a co-worker, Larry Bohn. I expressed feeling sorry about "The Flame" losing his job. He asked, "Would you hire him?" My answer was, "no." I didn't feel sorry for him after that. I think this was the only time I ever saw a direct hire let go!

Flaming idiot

I assumed responsibility for many of "The Flame's" screw-ups. In 1984, AMC had sold several hundred right-hand-drive Jeeps to the Post Office in Alaska. The steering gear bracket would develop cracks after about 5000 miles, it could fail and the vehicle could lose steering. No serious accidents occurred, primarily because of the diligence of the Post Office's mechanics in changing the brackets before anything could happen. Because the problem was a safety issue, it was AMC's and now Chrysler's obligation to fix it.

Dimwit had rounded up all the brackets in the parts system and had reinforcements welded to them. The brackets then failed at about 2000 miles, and the parts system was starting to get low. This was an illustrious demonstration of Eskelson's principle #1, "It's not what you don't know that gets you in trouble; it's what you know that ain't so!" The Flame "knew" the reinforcements would make the bracket stronger. "This ain't so;" the reinforcement caused the stresses in the bracket to be more highly concentrated, and the failures became more frequent.

We determined someone should visit Alaska to observe the conditions the Jeeps were being driven under. My new boss, who had replaced Mr. Steel, made the trip. He wasn't necessarily the most qualified to take the trip, but was an avid hunter and fisherman and consequently did not delegate the responsibility to someone more qualified. He came back and told me, "Yup, the brackets are breaking." He did enjoy the hunting and fishing!

Without any useful information from my new boss, I still came up with a solution. The bracket was originally "stamped;" a metal forming process common in the auto industry. The metal blanks (metal precut to fit in the stamping tools) are placed between two tools and squeezed with a tremendous force to shape the part. We needed to find the tools. This was an enormous task, because the parts had not been made for several years. We tracked down the tools and luckily, they had not been destroyed. We did

31

a run of parts with a stronger material than that of the original parts. I also designed an additional reinforcement strap to spread the load. We shipped the new brackets to Alaska and never heard from them again.

In another demonstration of Eskelson's principle #1; "The Flame" had a specification for what we called "steering wheel catch-up." In a power steering system, it is possible to turn the steering wheel faster than the power steering system's capability. "The Flame" thought he was "smarter" than the rest of the industry and specified there should never be a "catch-up" condition. Additionally, this expanded his authority to parts for which he did not have direct responsibility. His responsibility was the steering wheel and column. The no "catch up" specification also affected the power steering pump, hoses and gear. It required the power steering pump to be sized to pump more fluid than any other carmaker's pump. This resulted in extra fluid being pumped under pressure and more heat being generated. To handle the extra heat, cooling devices had to be used and power steering failures would occur more frequently. In addition, the steering effort for these vehicles became extremely light, causing the steering to feel vague; not a desirable characteristic. However, catch-up would never be experienced!

Apply the intelligent use of "principle #1" here, and you would say, "I don't know about power steering systems." With this attitude; the power steering pumps you would get from your expert supplier would have the same flow rate that your competitors also had. You would benefit from the supplier's or competitor's expertise based perhaps on someone at some time having good knowledge of such systems. Better steering feel would result, heat problems would not exist and a better vehicle would result. "The Flame" cost the corporation a lot of money because he knew better than anyone else.

Roger was always working on some letter to Francois Castaing (at AMC, everyone had access to him). He believed there were many more problems such as "catch-up," that needed to be corrected. The letters portended the doom of the corporation if action was not taken. These issues were out of Roger's area of responsibility. Other than my observation of Francois' typical French arrogance, he was no dummy and ignored Roger's rants. Roger thought he "knew" what was best. Most of it "wasn't so!" I can only think of one or two people I encountered in my career who were more delusional.

After "The Flame" was gone, I was doing some research about variable assist power steering systems because we wanted to reduce the power assist at higher speeds. Besides the over-assisted Cherokee, it was desirable to have less power assist at higher vehicle speeds, even on normal vehicles.

I shared some of the specifications of the Cherokee power steering system with suppliers who had some expertise in the field. The question as to why the flow rate was so high kept coming up. Eventually I learned it was because of "The Flame's" steering wheel catch-up specification. We changed the pumps to lower the flow and the steering feel on Cherokees improved.

I could probably write a book just about "The Flame" and his screw ups. As you can see, one person can do a lot of damage if he's an idiot and given some authority.

"Perfection is the Enemy of Good"

The experience with "catch-up" is not only a great illustration of Eskelson's "principle #1," but also an excellent example of the principle, "Perfection is the Enemy of Good," a quote from Bob Bachelor. This is a principle that has application in engineering and other areas of life. I worked with Bob for several years later in my career and learned most of what I know from him. Bob had been in the industry about 50 years when I hired on and had forgotten more than I'll ever know, and he still knew more than he'd forgotten. In the example of steering "catch-up," perfection in one area caused problems in many other areas. Too much of a "good" thing is <u>not</u> good. So much of the design process is trying to figure out how much of a "good" thing <u>is</u> good.

Flame thank you

I suppose I should thank "The Flame" for all his screw ups. He insured a bunch of us had work to do for many years. I wouldn't have become such an expert if I didn't have all those problems to solve. As good as the Cherokee was; it could have been so much better without "The Flame." Maybe without "The Flame's" services, AMC could have ridden the success of the Cherokee to later consume Chrysler. I can always speculate. Larry Bohn eventually became my manager. While in this position, he received "The Flame's" résumé from personnel. It highlighted Roger's many "accomplishments." Larry showed it to me; we did some editing, and had a good laugh.

Chapter 6

ALIGNMENT SPECIALIST

Vehicle alignment

The last process done to a car before shipping it to the dealer is adjusting the front end alignment. On a "quality" vehicle, alignment is the biggest warranty cost. Everything affects it, that is why it is done last. No one wants responsibility for the number one warranty issue. Stupid me took it on. Typically, four parameters are adjusted; steering wheel centering, caster, camber and toe angles. Following Eskelson's principle #1, I figured I knew nothing about alignment (despite my previous experience as a mechanic and on the mini-baja) and sought out those I thought might be experts. However, I did not get satisfactory answers to my questions. I did a lot of research on the subject and did some of my own experiments to better understand alignment. I discovered things contradicting what others were telling me. I became convinced no one else in the corporation understood alignment thoroughly. If someone once had, they'd since forgotten.

Dodge Van toe

The Dodge full size van was built across the river in Windsor, Ontario. It had a problem with the toe angle parameter of alignment. The van was an old design relatively unchanged since the early '70s, so the issue had been around awhile. These vans had a reputation for wearing tires out quickly and this issue was the reason why. Chrysler was undertaking measures to improve quality, so solving this issue became a "priority."

To insure the quality of the vans, a quality audit program was started. Random vehicles were subject to an audit in which several things were checked and measured. One of the things measured was alignment. The toe angle measurement consistently did poorly in the audit. The people at the assembly plant had learned in order to get the van to pass the audit; toe angle settings must be set out of the specifications. The majority of the vans, when measured in the audit, had toe angle that changed to within the specifications, and passed. Unfortunately, on about five percent of the vans, the toe angle setting didn't change and the vehicle failed the audit. No one understood why the toe angle changed on most and not on others, until I came along. I studied the problem for sometime before figuring it out.

In the assembly plant, the vans are supported in the air while workers put parts on them. The last thing put on the vans are the tires and then the vehicle is lowered to the ground. Then workers get in the van and drive it onto the alignment setting machine. Most are driven off the alignment machine and onto trucks or rail cars for shipping to dealers. A few were taken for audits. The time from when the tires were put on the van until it was driven onto the alignment machine, was about five minutes. However, when the assembly line stopped for a break, there were a few vans with the tires installed sitting on the ground, ready to be driven onto the alignment machine. These vans, depending on the length of the break, were on the ground with the weight of the vehicle on the tires for 30 minutes or longer. These vans were set out of the specification like all the others. When one of these was taken to the audit, it stayed out of specification and failed. Engineers at the assembly plant concluded something in the van was changing over time. They devised a method which attempted to accelerate the change. A very bumpy road was concocted in between the end of the assembly line and the alignment machine. It had no effect. I concluded the only factor which affected this change was "time." And the "time" seemed to be about 30 minutes.

I suggested the vans be parked for 30 minutes before setting the alignment. There was ample space to park the number of vans that are built in 30 minutes. This would allow whatever changes take place in the van to occur before alignment was set. To make this change required we only stop shipping vans for 30 minutes once. All vans could be set to specifications and would consistently pass the audit. Consistently passing the audit would mean a higher quality vehicle. If quality was a "priority" as Chrysler management had been preaching, the sensible thing would be to implement the change in processing immediately. Quality was not a priority! 30 minutes of production is worth perhaps $300,000. In a corporation where total sales are in the billions of dollars, they were not going to make a one time sacrifice of profits on $300,000 to provide a better quality vehicle. The reality is there are many opportunities to make up for 30 minutes in delayed shipments. After a few weeks no one would have ever noticed. Well, the common sense solution was not allowed, so I continued to study the problem. What could be changing over this period of time, and time being the only relative cause?

I spent some time standing underneath the assembly line, looking at the suspension parts making mental notes. I looked at the same parts on a van in the audit bay. A large rubber bushing in the front suspension was the culprit. The bushing in the van in the audit bay was a different shape than the ones on the assembly line. When the vans are supported in the air throughout assembly, there was no load on the bushing. As the van was completed and lowered to the ground, the weight of the vehicle caused a force of over 1000 lbs to bear against the bushing. The force caused the bushing to change shape over time, consequently changing the toe measurement.

A characteristic of rubber is when a force is applied to it; it will absorb the force as energy and push back. If the force is constant, it will lose its ability to push back over "time." Think of shooting a rubber band: stretching it puts energy into it. You release it and that energy propels the rubber band at your victim. You can probably repeat the exercise many times and the rubber band will continue to shoot. If you keep it stretched for 30 minutes before releasing it, it has no energy left and just falls to the ground and your victim is spared. If you repeatedly stretch and release the rubber band in quick succession, it will lose its ability to absorb energy similar to keeping a constant force on it. No matter the method, it must be done for a period of "time."

In the van, these same rubber principles apply. Initially, when the large force was applied to the bushing, it pushed back. Over "time," it lost this ability and then changed shape. When it changed shape, the toe setting also changed. The bushing was redesigned and the vans consistently passed the alignment audit. The new bushing was more expensive, so eventually the cost to the corporation of this fix was more than $300,000. The problem had existed for perhaps 15 years. I felt pretty cocky solving this.

Crooked steering wheels

At the Dodge Truck Plant in Warren, Michigan; the big issue was steering wheel centering (a crooked steering wheel). When a completed truck was driven onto the alignment machine, the driver attached a fixture to the steering wheel that would indicate when the steering wheel was straight. A signal light would turn on when the steering wheel was straight, and the driver would clamp the fixture in that position. Then, adjustments were made to straighten the two front tires (setting the toe parameter). One signal for each front tire would turn on when the tires had been adjusted to the specification. When all three signal lights were on, a gate opened allowing the vehicle to be driven off the machine. The driver unclamped the fixture on the steering wheel and drove the truck off to be shipped or occasionally taken for an audit. In the audit, a small percentage of the trucks had crooked steering wheels. The process had a finicky setting which should have insured straight steering wheels.

This only took one visit to the assembly plant to solve. To get an understanding of the process, I asked if I could drive a truck on the machine and set the fixture. I was curious to see how bad I could set the wheel and still turn on the signal light. I attached the fixture to the wheel and the light was lit (meaning the steering wheel is straight). I turned the wheel ¼ turn, and the signal stayed on. I wiggled some of the wires to the fixture that looked frayed, and the signal went out. Wiggling of the wires fixed a bad connection. I continued my experiment and disconnected the fixture from the machine, and the signal came on again. The engineers at the plant were embarrassed.

This was a problem. A bad connection to the fixture should have indicated something "bad." On the machine it indicated the setting for the steering wheel was good even when it was not. Bad vehicles got shipped. If the driver in the plant was lazy and didn't want to bother with the finicky setting, he could simply unplug the fixture and his life got easier. The design of the machine was changed, so if any of the fixtures or instruments failed, the vehicles would not be released.

Caster

Jeep Cherokees had alignment problems which were related to the "caster" parameter. "Caster" is not easily understood. I'll attempt to give you a basic understanding of what it is. Don't be discouraged if you don't understand it, nobody at Chrysler got it either.

When you turn the steering wheel of a car, it turns a gear, which then pushes on tie-rods. The tie-rods then turn the front tires to the left or right. When a front tire turns left or right, there is an axis that it will turn around. The axis is defined by components in the suspension and is also known as the kingpin or steering axis. The kingpin axis is nearly vertical or perpendicular to the road. "Caster" is the angle of the kingpin axis from vertical as viewed from the side of the car. Caster typical in the industry is 1 to 5 degrees.

The front of a bicycle also has caster. If you ride with no hands, the bicycle goes straight because of the effect of caster. When the bicycle is rolling, the weight of the bicycle and its rider cause a force to keep the wheel straight. It is the weight of the vehicle acting on the axis with "caster" that creates a force to keep the wheel straight. In a car, if you let go of your steering wheel, the car wants to go straight because of the same effect. In the bicycle, the angle from vertical is its "caster."

Now if you look at this axis from the front, its angle will be 0 degrees when the bicycle is going straight. What happens when you lean the bicycle while riding with no hands? The bicycle steers. It steers because the axis viewed from the front is no longer 0 degrees (the bicycle is leaned). In a vehicle, the kingpin axis is also tilted from vertical when viewed from the front. It is tilted in the side view, which we call "caster." The tilt in the front view is called Steering Axis Inclination (SAI). Note that it is the same axis! Just viewed differently.

I told you that "caster" in a vehicle will create a force which causes the wheels to go straight. This is not exactly true, because the kingpin axis is not only defined by "caster," it is also defined by "SAI." As with a leaning bicycle ridden with no hands, the vehicle's tires have a force that would cause them to steer left or right. They do not steer because the tie-rod in the steering system prevents it. The right tire on a vehicle wants to steer left due to the effect and the left tire wants to steer right. These forces result in the vehicle wanting to go straight, also known as the "center feel." Another benefit of this effect is that lash in the steering system is removed and steering is more precise. Ideally the steering forces at the front tires will be opposite and equal.

When I asked the so called experts what caster did, no mention of SAI was ever made. I was told more caster improved "center feel" and too much made steering efforts too high. From my research, no one understood the "steering" effect of these angles on the kingpin axis. When I asked about SAI I got blank stares. They did not seem to grasp that it was a different view of the same axis that caster defined. I did experiments and research to understand it further.

This may not be pleasant reading. I figure this is not difficult to understand, but then again, no one at Chrysler understood it except me. So if you understand it, you know more about it than anyone at Chrysler! This is one of those chapters about technology that I warned you about in the introduction. In *The Dilbert Principle*, Scott Adams states, "…it seems that a normal person would rather have a bushel of pine cones rammed up the nose than listen to a story about technology. But that's no reason to stop imparting valuable knowledge to a person who doesn't want it." So I continue.

On most vehicles, caster can be adjusted at each front wheel. SAI can be measured with most alignment equipment, but is not a parameter that is adjusted. It has a direct relationship to "camber." Camber is the plane in which the tire rotates. Don't worry if you don't understand that, most people at Chrysler don't. If "camber" is set properly, then SAI is correct.

Again, the two positive effects of the forces which results from caster and SAI are: the lash in the steering system is removed, making steering precise; and the forces from both wheels find a center and create the "center-feel." Increasing the caster angle increases the force and makes the center-feel stronger; a "good thing." At least this was the opinion of the ride and handling development engineers (the Vehicle Dynamics department). They had responsibility for deciding what caster should be.

It is not a perfect world in which we live. Due to "manufacturing variability," no two parts are ever made exactly alike, just like no two snowflakes are ever exactly alike. They can be very close though, that's what this "six-sigma" quality stuff is all about. As caster is increased, the forces which cause the tire to steer inward also increase. When these forces are greater, the possibility they will not be equal is also increased. When the forces are lower, differences are less perceptible. One side of the car may be heavier than the other, or the caster is not exactly equal (due to manufacturing variability, caster will never be "exactly" equal). The result when the force on one side of the vehicle is greater, is a steering pull to the right or the left in the vehicle. Not a good thing! An application of the "Perfection is the enemy of good" principle is shown here.

Improved or "perfect" center-feel increases the possibility of a steering pull. On "most" modern vehicles, provisions to adjust the caster are provided for. The caster can be adjusted on one side and the pull can be corrected. This is one reason why you would have an alignment done to your vehicle. With lower caster specifications, a steering pull is less likely due to variability, so it is less likely an alignment would be required. However, "steering feel" might be poor. The dilemma is how much of a "good" thing is good?

Cherokee Caster

When the Cherokee was designed, "The Flame" insured there would be one "good thing," no steering "catch up." Therefore, the power steering was "over boosted," and the vehicle had a poor "center feel." To improve the "center feel," the Vehicle Dynamics department specified caster for the Cherokee at 7 degrees (more than double the specification of most other vehicles). Much to their chagrin, the Cherokees built from 1984 until 1989, had been built with caster measuring about 4 degrees. At the lower caster number, the forces to steer the wheel inward were smaller and less likely to be out of balance, a good thing, mind you. However, this caused some problems.

First and not too serious, it was an opportunity for dealers to charge the corporation for warranty alignments. When a dealer received a new Cherokee, and it was out of specification; they would make the correction and send the bill to Chrysler. Every Cherokee was out of spec. Some dealers, wanting to deliver a quality vehicle to their customers would do an alignment under warranty on every vehicle they sold. This became quite expensive to Chrysler (number one warranty issue). The solution to the problem was not to pay for any warranty claims unless the end customer complained.

Dealers were not happy about this, it seemed we only cared about "profits" and not quality! Cherokees with lower caster never received any complaints (who would know to complain about caster anyway?). It would have been more beneficial just to change the specification. Dealers would still think we only cared about "profits," but no one else would have noticed. No customers were complaining.

In the assembly plant, when Chrysler began quality audits, the caster became a sore spot with the manufacturing engineers. The Vehicle Dynamics department had specified 7 degrees. The design of the Cherokee indicated caster should be 7 degrees. All the parts were to specification and yet caster would only measure at 4 degrees. This was baffling. I figured out the reason for the discrepancy.

Caster is not measured directly with an alignment machine. The wheels are steered to specific angles and camber is noted and then caster is calculated (remember, camber is directly related to the SAI which is the same axis that is caster). This is an effective method for measuring caster when it is less than 3 degrees (most cars). I discovered that when caster angles are larger, caster measurement with this method became very inaccurate. The vehicle would actually tilt and distort the camber measurements. So when the Vehicle Dynamics department requested the 7 degrees caster they had measured, it was actually closer to 11 degrees in the vehicle. I demonstrated to everyone interested that the Cherokee with 4 degrees caster actually had 7 degrees by design. It only was measuring 4 degrees. I recommended the specification just be changed, no customers were complaining. The Vehicle Dynamics department demanded this be corrected and Cherokees be built with caster that "measures" 7 degrees. It took about a year to implement the required changes. In 1989, all Cherokees were built with 7 degrees caster (11 by design) as measured. Problem solved, right? Remember, too much of a "good" thing is not good!

Beginning in 1989, a significant number of Cherokees were being bought back by the Corporation for a "steering pull" problem. When a customer has a complaint the manufacturer cannot resolve, the manufacturer can be forced to buy the vehicle back from the customer. When large numbers of vehicles are being bought back, the powers in the corporation want to know why. Why couldn't the "steering pull" be corrected? Cherokees have been built since 1984, why now on 1989 Cherokees?

In my discussion of caster and SAI, I informed you of a possible cause of steering pull: the steering forces resulting from the angles on the two kingpin axis are not equal. In 1989, with all the corrections made, Cherokees were built with 7 degrees caster as measured instead of 4 degrees. At the higher caster specification, it became more likely the forces causing the tires to steer were out of balance and "steering pull" resulted. So when the Cherokee had this pull, to fix it, just do an alignment, right? The Cherokee wasn't a modern vehicle. Caster adjustment on just one side of the vehicle was not easily accomplished! It required a cutting torch and a welder. The Jeep Link/Coil suspension did not provide for caster adjustment to be done on just one side of the vehicle. The front axle was one solid piece of steel welded together and an adjustment to one side adjusted the other. Thus the pull could not be corrected with an adjustment.

Because of the nature of the design of the Cherokee, the steering pull was always to the right. Typically, Cherokees had more weight on the left side of the vehicle. This caused the force at the left front tire (to steer to the right) to be greater than the force at the right front tire (to steer to the left). My solution was to increase caster on the right side of the vehicle (increasing the force to steer left) or to lower caster on the left (decreasing the force on the tire to steer right). Since it was not possible to adjust caster at a single wheel, I had several axles built purposely with caster up to 1 full degree higher on the right side (figuratively using a cutting torch and welder). Installing one of these axles would increase caster on just one side. With one of these axles installed, it corrected the steering pull. The problem with this fix was that it was very expensive; about $2000 per car. Chrysler management wanted a cheaper fix. There was not a cheaper fix found, and so nothing was done to correct it at that time. It was in the spring of 1990 when I introduced this fix.

French Ministry of Trade

Early October 1990, I was on a plane to France to fix steering pull on a Cherokee there. Cherokees in Europe sold for about twice what they did here. The Europeans thought of them like we think of a Mercedes, a premium vehicle. A customer in France had purchased one, and it had steering pull that could not be corrected, and Chrysler bought it back. The same customer, thinking it was a fluke and had bought a lemon, bought a second Cherokee, and likewise Chrysler bought it back. The customer really wanted a Cherokee and bought a third. He complained to the French Ministry of Trade when the third one had the same problem. The Ministry told Chrysler it would no longer allow Cherokees to be imported, until they could demonstrate that the steering pull could be corrected. Though they were not happy with my fix because of the expense, I was still the only one that had shown it could be fixed. Thus, I was on my way to France to fix it.

Fixing it was not hard; I'd already done it in Detroit. But getting my special axles to France was hard. I suppose Vehicle Development management believed in my genius and thought I could perform a miracle without the axles. I spent the majority of my time in France trying to solve the screw-up that prevented the axles from being delivered. When the proper axle finally arrived and was installed, the problem was corrected.

I satisfied the Ministry of Trade, and shipments of Cherokees continued to France. A permanent change to increase the caster on the right side of the axle was made at the supplier. The Vehicle Dynamics department would never admit their demand to have the higher caster had been the root-cause of the buy backs. (The actual root-cause was "the Flame's" steering catch-up specification, note the havoc wreaked by one idiot!) The vehicles built out of spec before 1989, didn't get bought back. The spec should have been changed as I had originally recommended, no customers were complaining. The axiom, "If it ain't broke, don't fix it" would have saved a bunch of trouble. With this experience, caster specifications for newer vehicle lines were lowered. With the introduction of the Grand Cherokee, the specification for the Cherokee was quietly reversed back as I had originally advised; allowing the Vehicle Dynamics department to save face.

Still solving it

Let me introduce you to *"Ever Workingonit,"* a member of the Vehicle Dynamics department. When I solved the steering pull problem, I lost interest in solving a problem I had already solved. Who wants to do a jigsaw puzzle twice? Don't answer that: I know there is some out there who do, but not me. Nevertheless, management was not happy with the solution. They wanted a no cost solution. This was not possible as demonstrated. I quit working on the problem and it became *Ever Workingonit's* career. He continued to gather data with all his test instruments on a Cherokee, hoping to find a cheaper solution. He produced many more stacks and stacks of data printouts, but never found another solution to solve the steering pull. It became his career, and I used to chuckle when I saw him driving the instrumented Cherokee around the proving ground months later.

He received great praise for his diligence from Chrysler management. I was called negative and lazy. What is productivity; solving a problem or killing a lot of trees? They didn't send him to France! Idiots.

Smoke and mirrors

Efforts were continually being made to reduce warranty costs. These efforts did not always involve solving the problem. Here is a more intelligent way:

I had a friend who had bought a brand new Chrysler convertible. The brake caliper had frozen and had damaged the rotor. The rotor, brake pads and caliper were replaced under warranty. She bought the same model the following year. The brake caliper froze on that one too. But the rotor was not covered by the warranty on the newer model; it was now considered a "wear" item! A stroke of the pen saved some warranty dollars here. Some areas of the car are easier to reduce warranty costs than others. I wish we had used this method on the Cherokee caster issue in the beginning.

Chapter 7

NEW BOSSES

AMC takes over

At the time of the merger in 1987, AMC was working on the design of the Grand Cherokee. Chrysler was designing a similar sized SUV based on the Dakota (prompted by the success of the Cherokee and a few years late). The Dakota design was dropped in favor of the Grand Cherokee. The Dodge Intrepid was more closely related to the Eagle Premier than the K-car. The new Dodge Ram Trucks had a Jeep style front suspension. Engineering departments were reorganized into an AMC fashion. Internally, it was said to be patterned after Honda. After the first few years, it looked as if AMC had taken over Chrysler. Don't be fooled, the Chrysler culture (huge egos and poor management) came to dominate the new organization and productivity slowed.

In the late '70s, Chrysler had decided to get out of the truck business. They stopped building large trucks, motor home chassis, dropped the 440 engine, etc. They intended to continue the pick-up trucks and full-size vans until the tools wore out. Both had been designed in the early '70s and had continued with minor changes until the merger with AMC. With the success of the compact pick-up trucks in the '80s, Chrysler had a midsize copy in the Dakota (they contracted the design to an outside design house). Chrysler had become the minivan and K-car company; they didn't know how to design anything else. Since facing bankruptcy, Chrysler had not invested in research, and their products were rapidly becoming obsolete.

The merger with AMC brought Chrysler back to life. It seemed to me that AMC taught Chrysler how to design cars again. In fact, many of the AMC brain trust had been former Chrysler Employees, who had taken early retirement when Chrysler faced bankruptcy in the early eighties. After the merger, the design of the Jeeps remained with the former AMC engineering group. The aging Dodge truck products and the Dakota were added to these responsibilities. The AMC car products were transferred to the Chrysler engineering team, which when the "Appliance" was dropped, was essentially the Eagle Premier. We became Jeep and Truck Engineering (JTE). Chrysler Engineering became Passenger Car (Pass Car)

Engineering and took responsibility for minivans and cars. The staffing at JTE was about 1/10th of that at Pass Car. This hardly seemed fair, considering more than half the vehicles Chrysler manufactured were Jeeps and trucks. Francois Castaing stayed on as the Chief at JTE.

Looking elsewhere

Being so short staffed, I was quite discontent with things and on several occasions I sought employment elsewhere. Once a headhunter had nearly convinced me to take a job with a seat supplier; promising me a significant increase in salary. When we met to seal the deal, the offer was for the same salary as I was already making, so I declined. The Chief Engineer of our department, Don Buhler, did express he valued my work. This was influential in my decision to decline the offer.

I once flew to Marysville, Ohio and interviewed with Honda. In the interview, they seemed uninterested in my skills, but were diligent in trying to determine if I would work 52 hour weeks without being paid overtime. I became irritated as I was passed around from person to person with the same experience. It was a big turn-off. As I was leaving, they asked me directly if I was interested in the position, I responded, "I'm a red blooded American, offer me enough money, I'd be interested." I wasn't given an offer.

Misfits

When Tom Steel went to Passenger Car Engineering, my co-worker Larry Bohn lobbied hard to be his replacement. But Larry was thought of as a "loose canon" and another was selected. Let's call him *"Dave Drunk."* No one had ever heard of him, but his previous manager had given him a "glowing" performance review. I guess it was easier than firing him. He had an alcohol problem at the time, and was my boss for the next year and a half. When he was in, you would have to catch him before lunch, because he often didn't come back. He habitually called in sick 1-2 times a week. In fact, I only recall one week when he showed up all five days. It really ticked me off that he went to Alaska instead of me. In an intelligent situation, I suppose he would have been fired after just a few months. Chrysler was afraid to fire any direct employees. He eventually resigned after being pressured to do so.

Valuing engineers

Dave's replacement was the known quantity, Larry Bohn. My complaint about Larry is that meetings were lengthy because he wouldn't shut up. Despite this flaw, he was the greatest boss to work for. Every performance review was surprisingly praising. Every raise was larger than expected. Not just with me, but with all of his subordinates. As soon as it was possible within corporate guidelines, he had me promoted. He was the only manager that ever had me promoted. He was always supportive. Because of his "loose cannon" style, he left Chrysler before I did. After I had transferred out of his department, his name occasionally came up in a derogatory manner, and I always came to his defense.

Overtime

With the skeleton staffing levels at JTE, there wasn't much "slow time" like there had been at GM. Instead of 20 minutes of work a day, there was 5-6 hours of work; still not enough to require me to work overtime. Less competent engineers typically needed to work overtime to stay on top of their responsibilities and it became desirable to make additions to the staff. But because I wasn't working overtime, a case for more staffing was difficult to make, so I was asked to work overtime. I did for awhile, but I didn't like the place that much and didn't continue at it for long. A co-worker, Randy Johnson who worked a lot of overtime, told me, "Evan, you need to get married, then you won't want to go home, and you'll want overtime." I'm afraid I wasn't very helpful to my managers who wanted to expand the size of their staffs. I hope Randy's wife doesn't read this.

The Juice

The organization of our Engineering Department consisted of an Executive Engineer at the top, he reported to the Engineering VP. Chief Engineers over the Drive train and Chassis departments reported to this executive. Also reporting to the Executive Engineer were the managers of the labs and of the draftsmen. Our Executive Engineer's first initials were the same as a famous former running back, thus we called him the *"Juice"* when he wasn't present. He had no personality and brought a manager with even less personality with him from his former position as Chief Engineer of AMC's scientific labs. Nevertheless, he was a trendsetter. He was the first to name a conference room after himself, an action that would have destroyed his career at AMC, but Chrysler considered it progressive.

I'm sure you are all aware (not!); shortly before the merger with Chrysler, a Jeep Comanche set a new land speed record for a pickup truck at the Bonneville Salt Flats (you can invent any classification you want and set a record). Internally at Jeep and Truck Engineering, much was made of this feat, but actually I think it was the first time such a record was attempted with a pickup truck classification. The *Juice's* underling and the underling of this underling were the only ones ever allowed to drive this special truck. With this glowing success, *Juice* promoted his underling to be the manager of the department's labs. The underling was such a prick, that it eventually led to a near mutiny of all those who worked in the labs.

To solve the problem, the underling was promoted to a specialist with no one reporting to him as no one could stand to work with him. He was given research assignments and could delude himself into thinking he was doing something very important. He rarely bothered anyone after that. He still provided a lot to laugh about though. He was given an office like a manager. When he went off to meet with someone; he would post a hand written dissertation on several pages of yellow notepad paper on his door explaining his whereabouts (as if he thought somebody cared or would be looking for him).

I thought this was an effective way to deal with such a misfit; little did I know it was a common way for Chrysler to deal with misfits. "Assign them to research." Too bad AMC didn't have had such a method to deal with "The Flame."

Chapter 8

AN INNOVATOR

4 wheel steer

Shortly after the merger with Chrysler, Francois Castaing was anxious to demonstrate the competence of the AMC staff to his new Chrysler bosses. This led to the *Juice* directing us to develop a 4-wheel steering system for the full-size Dodge van. And to make it extra difficult, it had the requirement to be a mechanical system (no electronics or hydraulics, technologies that would have been more promising). We were given a time frame of about two months to demonstrate a prototype to Bob Lutz, Castaing's boss. The two months time frame included the Holiday season. It seemed it was a doomed project from the start. Because I wasn't working overtime, I was assigned to it.

As with the Mini-Baja project in college, I informally became the project manager. We demonstrated a prototype to Mr. Lutz three months later. Mr. Lutz delayed several times his visit to JTE, thus buying us extra time. Unlike in college, I had the assistance of many competent people. Brainstorming with my future boss Larry Bohn, a control mechanism was invented. The designer Tom Johnson used the latest in CAD software to design the control mechanism and further refine it. The designer Gerry Hennesy fit the parts in the vehicle. The technician Doug Farr adapted the vehicle and offered many suggestions that improved the design. As soon as it became apparent we would have a vehicle to demonstrate to Mr. Lutz, the *Juice* wanted a more active roll in the design and we had some disagreements. He ordered me to make a design change to the control mechanism which I thought ridiculous. You could say I was insubordinate, because I didn't follow his orders.

It was a fun project, but we came to the conclusion that though it was feasible, it was expensive, the benefit was not worth the cost. Maybe we were wrong. GMC has been advertising a 4-wheel steering system on a full size pick-up truck lately (they use electronics, the dummies). We were just ahead of our time.

The project did cast a positive light on the department, and therefore the *Juice*'s underlings wanted to bask in the glory too. They took over and insured the death of the project. The *Juice* never spoke directly to me again.

Tools of the trade

As I have mentioned before, I had responsibility for front end alignment. In solving the many alignment issues, I became the "alignment expert" at JTE. My efforts on these alignment issues knocked them off their perch as number one in warranty cost. Our vehicles were not "quality" vehicles, so other issues took over this mantle. As the alignment expert, I was given the task to write the processing standards for setting alignment at the assembly plants for all Jeeps and Dodge trucks. These standards were still being followed when I left Chrysler.

As the alignment expert, it was my desire to have a machine which measured alignment in our department's lab. Oh, you assumed we already did. Lest you forget, this was Chrysler; "common sense" was not common!

There are several manufacturers of alignment measuring machines. I begged, cried, had tantrums, and threatened to quit, all to no avail; the *Juice* always nixed it. "Other departments had alignment machines. We didn't need one." "Was alignment their responsibility?" I would retort. We had to schedule way in advance to get an appointment on one of those machines. Then we were not free to do tasks we had not planned when we didn't the get results we expected. This greatly hampered studies in solving certain alignment issues. I was continually told there was no capital budget to pay for it.

Dummy me! I believe I possess an uncommonly large amount of "common sense." So much so, that sometimes it takes me a while to tap into it. "We're a huge car company." All I had to do was ask one of the manufacturers of said alignment machines, and they would lend us one. I could have had one months earlier. I asked and we had an alignment machine installed in our lab. The technicians hated it, because they used it so often after they got it. After the *Juice* had denied my request for an alignment machine many times, he walked in the lab one day, saw it, and threw a fit. I'm sure that would have been the end of my career right then, except we hadn't paid a cent for it.

Virtual tools

At the time, the usage of CAD technology was becoming widespread at Chrysler. AMC had adopted the CATIA program that had been developed in Europe by Dassault for the Airbus. Chrysler had been developing its own CAD system. A team was organized to evaluate the two systems and make a recommendation as to which system the whole of Chrysler should adopt. Rumor has it the team recommended the Chrysler system, but a relative of Mr. Castaing was an executive at Dassault, and CATIA was selected. Mr. Castaing had managed to become the VP of Vehicle Engineering and had the authority to make such an important decision.

In my years at Chrysler, I had a vision of finding better ways to design cars and a desire to design better cars (lazy butt that I was). When new technology became available, I was usually the first to embrace it. I imagined we could learn to build a virtual car on the computer, thus eliminating much of the testing and prototyping. My first foray into this technology was in the engine department with my attempt to simulate intake manifold airflow on a computer. This first attempt of mine was a failure, but it didn't stop me from making subsequent attempts.

I was instrumental in the first applications of new technology in the design process in several areas. The first was on the design of the 4-wheel steering mechanism. An enhancement to CATIA called "Kinematics" had been released shortly before the 4-wheel steer project. "Kinematics" allowed the virtual parts to be moved around in the virtual space of the computer. No one was trained on it at the time; nevertheless I was current on such topics and knew it was available. I encouraged Tom Johnson to use "kinematics" in the development of our 4-wheel steering control. As far as I know, he was the first to apply "kinematics" in the design process. Several years later when I was trained in kinematics, the steering control was an example project in the class.

One of the other departments demonstrated a new prototyping technology called "stereolithography." A computer design of a part could be converted to a "solid" model, and then a mock-up of it in plastic could be produced in a matter of hours. Normally the process to mock up a part was done by hand and took several weeks. The *Juice,* upon learning of this technology, forbade us from using it. He deemed our designers did not have the time to convert the computer models to a solid. Insubordinate and lazy as I was, I used this new technology in a part for the new Grand Cherokee. As far as I know this was the first part used in production where stereolithography was used in the design process. And the *Juice* was not happy with me, and I fell further from grace.

Chapter 9

AUTHORITY ALWAYS WINS

Formal vs. informal authority

Somewhere in my career I heard a lecture discussing authority. Formal authority was the power of your position. Informal authority was the power of your competence. A competent person can get people to do work for them, because the people know the competent person will not waste their time. A leader with both types of authority will be very effective. At the time, I had little formal authority, but I was very competent and noticed I never had trouble getting technicians or designers to do work for me. I chalked this up to informal authority and didn't feel an urgent need for formal authority.

The purpose of the lecture was to get those with formal authority to work harder at obtaining informal authority to make them more effective leaders. The *Juice* lacked informal authority; with my informal authority, I ran the 4-wheel-steer project with little interference from him. The prototype got built quickly and a demonstration was made. Without formal authority, the project was taken away and given to the *Juice*'s underlings. They did not accomplish much with their formal authority. It was my opinion; more is accomplished with informal authority. The lesson I didn't learn at the time, and appears I never learned; is informal authority is never enough! To ultimately be successful, at least a little formal authority is required in addition to informal authority.

The *Juice* was not the only executive I butted heads with. Ok, there were a lot. The *"Go-Cart"* was the manager of the Vehicle Dynamics department. The moniker *"Go-Cart"* was assigned to him, because it seemed it was his desire to have all our vehicles handle like go-carts, and it rhymed with his real name. Go-carts have very quick steering (the Jeep Wrangler had the same overall steering ratio of a Corvette). It made the vehicles "fun-to-drive", but also increased the likeliness of loosing control in emergency maneuvers -- an application of the "Perfection is the Enemy of Good" principle. With the fixing of the Cherokee steering pull problem, I suppose the *Go-Cart* felt a little humiliated because his department could not fix it, but I had. In fact, they had been the cause of the problem; because they couldn't

51

even follow the simple principle; "if it ain't broke, don't fix it." They had demanded Cherokees be built with 7 degrees caster, when no customers were complaining about any issues that result from lower caster.

It seemed the *Go-cart* often tried to retaliate and humiliate me in some large meeting. Before the meeting started he would demand some stupid design change that affected my responsibility. I would shoot back with facts illustrating the stupidity of his demands. During the meeting, he said little, knowing I was prepared to fire back if he opened his mouth again. Then he said nothing to me until the next meeting, and the scenario would repeat. He had been promoted to Chief Engineer and it seemed to get worse. My informal authority (competence and good sense) stood up to the *Go-Cart*, and he often looked the fool in these confrontations, when I returned his verbal assault with facts.

Formal authority

Because steering and suspension parts were deemed "safety parts", engineers responsible for these parts had certain formal authority that engineers for non-safety parts did not. I had formal authority on some of these parts.

Most parts for an automobile are manufactured by smaller companies called suppliers. On non-safety parts, the Chrysler Purchasing Department had the authority to select the supplier. On safety parts, the engineer had the authority to select the supplier. Often the Purchasing Department forgot about this and tried to dictate the supplier on such safety parts.

In the Early '90s, Chrysler was once again struggling financially. The entire product line was aging and heavy incentives were used to entice buyers. Many new models (more than restyled K-cars) were nearing introduction. We believed these new models would be successful and return the corporation to profitability. Until the new products were introduced, cost cutting measures of all sorts were rampant to get us through those tough times. The VP of Purchasing issued an edict that froze the prices we paid suppliers for parts. Most suppliers conformed because they desired to keep selling parts to Chrysler.

There were a few exceptions. A small company in upstate New York supplied a small rubber steering part, which was used in the Dodge Ram 4-wheel drive trucks. The number of this model truck built each day was relatively small (less than 100 a day). The rubber compound was proprietary to this small company. It was used in a harsh environment and had to pass strict tests. The company requested a price increase that amounted to about $4000 a year. The Chrysler purchasing department flatly refused the price increase based on the VP's edict. Unfortunately for Chrysler, this was the only part the company sold to Chrysler. They said they would just stop making the part if Chrysler would not pay the higher price. No other pressure could be used against the company. Our purchasing agent came to me and demanded I find a new supplier. She informed me Chrysler would not tolerate any price increases.

The process of selecting a new supplier, particularly when the material is proprietary, is not easy. Parts must be prototyped, then thoroughly tested in a lab, and then tested in a vehicle at the Proving Grounds. The selection of a new supplier would cost the corporation at least $20,000, probably much more. Spending $20,000 to save $4,000 seemed to defeat the purpose of the VP's edict. If this vehicle model was to be produced for five more years, it might make sense in the long run. However, this model was slated to be replaced in less than two years. I informed the purchasing agent we would not be selecting a new supplier because of the aforementioned reasons. The agent then threatened me, "What are you going to do when the truck assembly plant shuts down because they run out of these parts?" I returned the threat, "What are *you* going to do when the plant shuts down because they run out of these parts?!" I lost my temper and verbally berated the purchasing agent for a good five minutes. Well, atypical to what usually happens in a large corporation, purchasing paid an extra $4,000 that year instead of spending $20,000 in selecting a new supplier. The plant kept running. Sometimes, formal authority can be put to good use.

Defective safety parts

Steering tie-rod ends contain a ball and socket joint. The ball part is on the end of a threaded stud. If any of these parts were to fail, the vehicle could lose steering and cause a serious accident, thus "safety parts." To insure the integrity of the ball-stud part, 100 percent of the parts were x-rayed. However, not always did someone look at all of the x-rays.

The supplier of the part informed us they had discovered a small number of defective parts. Some had been installed in components that had been shipped to our assembly plant. A significant amount of time had passed since receiving the shipments. In order to insure all vehicles with defective parts were found, a major recall might be required. The supplier immediately started testing on the defective parts they had recovered. Failures of defective parts in the tests were almost immediate. Some did not fail and passed the entire test for durability. Additionally, vehicles were tested with broken parts. With the caster effect on the tires, the vehicles could be safely stopped when a problem with the steering was noted by the driver.

Based on these test results, the team assembled to address the issue concluded; if the parts were to fail in the field, it would have already happened. A recall would likely not serve any purpose. I was a part of the team. We kept no notes. We never met again on the subject.

When safety parts fail, people can be killed. So much care is done to insure the integrity of these parts. The system broke down in this case. From our testing, we concluded there was nothing we could do further to save someone's life if one of these had been installed in a car. So we quietly never talked about it again and hoped that no one would ever get hurt because of it.

Graft

With the authority to select suppliers, engineers were showered with graft. Besides pocketknives, calendars and pens; they bought us lunch, threw Christmas parties, sporting events tickets, and more. The best seats I ever had at a Tigers game were from a supplier. Seven rows behind home plate. Some engineers worked very hard to get suppliers to buy them lunches, some everyday. Chrysler at times tried to stem the practice as it did little to insure integrity in the supplier selection process.

Many of the engineers liked going to Gentlemen's (strip) clubs. Not me. Accordingly I was quite naive when it came to these situations. One supplier threw a party in Canada (10 minutes away across the river) every year. I was asked if I would like to go. They were going to the "Ballet." I wasn't particularly enamored with ballet, however seeing an opportunity for a cheap date; I asked if I could take a date. "No, the Canadian Ballet!" Strip clubs in Canada had no clothing requirements, and were known as the "Canadian Ballet." Someone had to explain it to me. I then declined.

Perks

There were other perks. Company vehicles could be driven home overnight, and the company bought the gas. Unless you were someone real important, you were not supposed to do this more than once or twice a month. Another thing nice about the company vehicles was, when traveling to another Chrysler facility, you could pull right in the facility to park. If you take your own vehicle, you parked in the visitor's lot and walked a long way. At various times in my career, I had responsibility for specific vehicles which had experimental parts installed on them. I would pass them around to various people for evaluation. Sometimes I drove them home myself.

Some people were more abusive of the perk. One such person was *"Two-Beards,"* also known as the *"Tetris King."* Personal Computers (PCs) were starting to show up on more than just the secretaries' desks. One was placed in each aisle among the engineer's cubicles. They were primarily used to play computer games during lunch. And *Two-Beards* was the best. It is funny to note, that though *Two-Beards* had the quickest reflexes which enabled him to play at a much higher level than any of the rest of us; he could never outscore me, because I knew some scoring secrets to get bonus points that I did not share with him. This frustrated *Two-Beards* immensely as it seemed his definition of being a man was to have the high score on Tetris. Someone finally filled him in on the secrets and he was untouchable.

I let *Two-Beards* take home the vehicle I was responsible for at the time, and I couldn't find him for a week. One day, I had a meeting at an assembly plant. As visitor parking spots at the plant were scarce, I hunted him down and took the keys from him. He had his laundry in the car, among other things. I wouldn't be able to get through security at the assembly plant with laundry in the car, so I threw it out on the ground and drove off. He complained to our boss that my treatment of him had been harsh, nevertheless he found no sympathy. This was one of only a few times in my career when I lost my temper. I was known for always possessing a cool head. So if I had lost it with him, my boss thought he probably deserved it.

Performance reviews

In the politically correct environment of the '90s, it no longer became important that you knew what you were doing and that you got it done. This was only a small factor. More important was how you made those you work with "feel," that you valued "diversity" and you did not create a "hostile" workplace for your co-workers. In all my performance reviews over the years, my competence and job knowledge were never questioned. However, I was encouraged to make improvements in these politically correct areas.

Dale Carnegie training was the popular way for one to make improvements in some of these areas. The company would pay for it. I disagreed the training was important. Those I had known who had taken the training, just seemed more insincere and smiled a lot more when they were lying. So when I learned I would have to take the class on my own time, I declined. Bad move, I suppose.

King Lido

I never met Lee Iacocca, but once I was able to have my picture taken with a full size cardboard cutout of Him. I also got to watch Him on a video that was for employees only. His actions and decisions did have some effect on me, so I will write a little about Him. At Chrysler He was regarded as Royalty. When He declined to run for president, I think He did so, viewing the presidency as a demotion from his current "deity" status. I only remember Him making one visit to Jeep and Truck Engineering. The main hall where He would be walking through to the rear of the building was cordoned off, and security guards watched each door. We had to use the other halls until He left the building.

Lee was a master marketer. He persuaded many Americans to buy crappy cars. The K-cars were cheap and very short (so more of them could be crammed into a rail car to save on shipping costs). A five year warranty was offered and Lee got America to buy so many that Chrysler paid off the government loan years early. The success of the minivan also helped.

After the design on these two successful products was completed, early retirements were offered to Chrysler's brightest. The truck lines were headed for extinction. All Chrysler had to offer was stretched and other variants of the K-car (minivans included). The people who could design new products had left and most had gone to work at AMC. Lee's decisions initially saved Chrysler. But with aging products, he put Chrysler back on the path to extinction.

Customer research indicated the top two reasons for buying a Chrysler were, low cost and warranty. People were becoming more affluent and weren't looking for cheap cars anymore. The merger with AMC slowed Chrysler's progress to extinction. The Jeeps added a premium product to Chrysler's offerings. Talent to design cars was brought (bought?) back. New products were needed. Jeep carried them until new products could be introduced. The AMC people were unleashed and exciting new vehicles dominated the early '90s and Chrysler was "saved" again by Lee Iacocca.

In reality, Lee reluctantly gave approval for these new products after his underlings impressed upon him they were required to head off declining sales. An ad slogan of Chrysler at the time preached, "Lead, follow or get out of the way." Lee applied this and got out of the way. He had been leading us to extinction again. He still didn't budget for research. Instead he took a big salary and left before things went bad again. In the end, his mismanagement resulted in the demise of Chrysler. To be fair, Chrysler was headed for extinction before he came on board, and perhaps he did slow the demise by a decade or two. A true leader would have preserved the corporation. It had adequate resources and could have been saved.

Chapter 10

SPECIAL ORGANIZATIONS

Liberty Organized

After Lee's "masterful" leadership of the company out of the verge of bankruptcy, he was selected to head up the project to restore the Statue of Liberty. GM had announced the formation of Saturn, which was supposed to re-invent how cars are made. Ford had announced a similar research project. It's rumored that while in New York, a reporter inquired of Mr. Iacocca if Chrysler had a similar project. Chrysler did not, but Lee wouldn't admit it and told the reporter we had the "Liberty" project. On his next trip to Detroit (he was spending a lot of time in New York as a "celebrity" at the time), an "expendable" (or "stupid" as I would say) executive was found and the Liberty team was formed.

My last position with Chrysler before I resigned was with the Liberty team. I suppose the stupidity I observed at Liberty is the highlight of this book. GM's Saturn eventually became a GM division which made pricey economy cars. Liberty was created on a whim of Lee's, and so remained. Liberty's research efforts never contributed to Chrysler's benefit. After working at Liberty, I shared this observation with some of my peers, and they claimed Liberty had done the preliminary design work on the electric minivan. The electric minivan did not make a profit for the corporation, so I can make the argument that it was of no benefit. An argument could be made that Liberty had a public relations benefit? Hmm…, Lee's specialty.

Viper staffed

In the few years I'd been with Chrysler, I had become the expert in a few areas of vehicle design. On occasion, I was called upon to assist in solving problems for other departments. The Dodge Viper show car was a hit at the Detroit Auto Show. The decision was made to go to production with it. Well as you can imagine, every engineer including yours truly wanted to be part of the Viper team. Chrysler decided to use this enthusiasm to save money in the design of the Viper. The team would be made up of engineers that wanted to work after hours on the project gratis. I wasn't that enthusiastic about it. Those who did were wannabes. When these wannabes screwed things up in areas I was expert in, I was consulted. I remember being consulted about the steering intermediate shaft for the Viper. The method of staffing the Viper team resulted in numerous delays in its introduction. Many problems with the vehicle needed to be resolved. Not very bright people were designing it.

An example is the Viper frame. The original material selected for the frame was pre-treated to resist corrosion. The material is difficult to weld, and the welds looked awful. With the amount of welding done on the frame, the corrosion treatment of the material was ruined, so the finished frame was run through an E-dip process to provide it with corrosion protection. Now if this is starting to sound silly to you, you know what I was thinking. I suggested using a non-treated material for the frame that would weld easily, and then do the E-dip process. This would result in a frame without the awful looking welds and the same corrosion protection. Some of the early Vipers were built with the awful looking frame, fortunately the body hides it. Shortly after I made this verbal suggestion, the Viper frame process was changed. I doubt I was ever given credit, they probably didn't even remember my name.

Advanced design

The Advanced Vehicle Packaging (AVP) department was responsible for the preliminary design of future products. They would work on the design up until about two years before production. Then, the design responsibility would be given to the product engineering groups for the final design, supplier selection and release for production. The AVP department often built prototype vehicles to test out new designs. We thought of the people in AVP as a bunch of idiots, it seemed we had to completely redesign everything they did.

On one of their projects, AVP came to me for advice on how to solve a problem. In an early prototype of the new Ram pickup they had designed a suspension with a spring between the steering column and the steering gear. Idiots! The shaft going between the column and the gear is called an intermediate shaft. I was the intermediate shaft expert at the time. I designed a shaft to snake around the spring with three joints in it with a support bearing, and the problem was solved. I deemed this a stupid design and emphasized that even though it will work on the one prototype, never would it be acceptable for production. This suspension design was not adopted for the final design (maybe because of the stupid intermediate shaft), and I was glad. Irregardless, stupid me, I could have patented the design (see my discussion about patents later in the book) and could have gotten a big patent bonus. The design was later used in production on the

'97 Jeep Wrangler.

Bigger fish

Our department had responsibility for products that fit into two categories: vehicles already in production and vehicles nearing production (just handed off from AVP). Most of the problems I solved were on vehicles already in production -- somebody else's screw-up. The one vehicle I worked on that was nearing production was the Grand Cherokee. It was nearly the same as the Cherokee, so we were able to ward off the problems which the Cherokee had experienced. I selected suppliers and no big issues needed to be resolved.

In the three and a half years I was in the steering and suspension design department at JTE, I changed responsibilities several times. My manager, Larry Bohn, changed my responsibilities again saying, "You are so far ahead that if you did nothing for two years, nothing would go wrong." My previous design responsibility was passed on to a more novice engineer and I assumed responsibility for power steering hoses, pumps etc. The only thing I remember doing with this responsibility is traveling to three parts plants where various hoses were made. The trip was two days and in four states on a corporate jet.

Larry did not understand the "laziness" principle. I had worked myself out of a job by fixing all the problems with alignment and intermediate shafts. I didn't do this so I would have time to now work on power steering stuff, as flattering as it was. It was a complement to be assigned the new duties. However, I would rather relax a little and enjoy the fruits of my labors and not be so stressed -- like when I finished the blueprints two days early, I figured I deserved to go golfing those days. With my new assignment, I specialized with the hydraulic part of the steering system. I was confident I could design these parts, but was also confident in my abilities to design the entire steering and suspension systems. I became just a little curious about whether there was an opportunity in which I could use all the talents I had acquired.

Retiring

Bob Bachelor was approaching his third retirement with Chrysler in the AVP department, and they were looking for a replacement. He wasn't very old, contrary to what you would imagine when someone retires three times. However he had been with Chrysler so long, that he remembered working with one of the original Chrysler engineers, Zeder, Skelton or Breer (the design team that designed the very first Chrysler automobile). To be eligible for retirement at Chrysler, you had to have 30 years of service if you were under age 60. If you had 10 years of service and were age 60 or over, you were also eligible. Bob had started with Chrysler when he was so young that he would be eligible for his first retirement before age 50. Bob passed away at age 71, about two years after his third retirement.

If you are doing the math, it won't work out. Put your calculators away while I explain this. Beginning with the great depression, Chrysler had a habit of facing bankruptcy about every ten years. In those times, early retirements were offered to employees that had not yet become eligible for retirement. Somehow this was a cost savings measure (I don't understand how this saves a corporation money to pay people to not work?). Often these "early" retirement packages were very attractive. "Early" means that it is offered before one is eligible. Bob took one of these packages and retired early, before age 50. Chrysler survived this brush with bankruptcy (because they were paying people to not work?). When the good times returned, they realized they needed Bob's expertise and brought him back (when Bob receives a pension plus a salary, how is this saving Chrysler money?).

When Chrysler had their most famous brush with bankruptcy in the early eighties, Bob had put in another 10 years. Though not age sixty yet, he was offered another very lucrative early retirement package. He retired a second time and was collecting two pensions. He did not ever need to work again. In retirement, Bob was bored. Many of his fellow retirees had joined AMC. As Bob put it, "if they give me interesting work to do, I'll stay with it." He joined AMC too. When Chrysler merged with AMC, he was once again a Chrysler employee. After 10 years with AMC and Chrysler, he retired a third time, and not early this time.

The real minivan story

I had the opportunity to hear many stories from Bob. Before his second retirement, he had been instrumental in the development of the Chrysler Minivan introduced in 1983 as a 1984 model. Chrysler historians will tell you the Minivan's phenomenal success was always in their plan. This is why you want the story from me; I'll tell you Bob's version. It was actually quite an accident that Chrysler's minivan became as successful as it did. It was the clever application of Eskelson's principle #3 by Chrysler that created it. It was GM and Ford's refusal to apply the principle that made it Chrysler's most successful product ever.

The original idea was to downsize the full size van, similar to many cars that were downsized in the '70s. Over at Ford Motor Company, Hal Sperlich had been promoting an idea for a minivan, which he touted would likely be a replacement for station wagons. The idea failed to get traction at

Ford. Station wagons were not selling well. In Europe and Japan, minivans were already being manufactured. These versions were not particularly popular in their own markets. Sperlich had enough "formal authority" at Ford that some prototypes were designed and built. Mr. Ford would not approve the program. He didn't believe there was a market for them based on the market for station wagons and the foreign models mediocre success.

Hal was fired by Iacocca at Ford and came to Chrysler. Rumor has it that when Lee agreed to join Chrysler sometime later, he took one of Ford's prototype minivans and drove it to a secret Chrysler facility where Chrysler personnel could thoroughly examine it. The final Chrysler design was based on the Ford prototype. Lee returned the minivan to Ford and came to work at Chrysler. Unlike other minivans in the world, this one was front wheel drive and had no bumps or humps in the driver and passenger space.

Generally, when a car company designs a new car, it is desirable to use parts that you already manufacture. This saves a lot of money in development costs. Chrysler did not have front wheel drive parts that would work on a vehicle this size. Bob Bachelor with many others, like those at GM and Ford, thought the minivan should be rear wheel drive. Why spend the money to design all new parts? The new K-car, which was front wheel drive, was being designed at the time. Hal Sperlich was adamant it be front wheel drive and got his way. The front wheel drive parts were mostly adapted from the K-car design.

Chrysler's original plans were to have the new minivan replace the full size van. Initial production called for a large percentage to be work vans, with no back or side windows and no seats behind the driver. They didn't sell very many. However, with no bumps or humps in the passenger compartment, sales took off on the versions with windows and seats. It's a convenience thing; other minivans had humps and bumps, and station wagons were even worse. People loved the minivan. Ford and GM thought they would have similar success when they introduced their rear wheel drive versions with a big engine hump out of the dashboard. People didn't like the hump! The minivan became Chrysler's most successful vehicle ever. It was a design stolen from Ford. This would make Eskelson proud! In principle #3, "Don't be too proud to steal another's idea, it is a lot less trouble."

Chrysler was the number three automaker. Ford and GM could have easily copied the Chrysler minivan and taken a big chunk of the market. Ford and GM refused. They would not "flatter" Mr. Iacocca with their own imitations. So Chrysler was left to profit for many years without any serious competition.

As a side note, businesses kept buying the full size van, the minivan was too small.

Replacing Bob

AVP was looking for a replacement for Bob, and I applied for the position. It seemed a good fit for me and would use more of my talent. In fact, it was the same position that I had applied for years earlier when I originally interviewed with AMC. The manager then was Chris Teddy; shortly after that interview he had been promoted to an executive position, resulting in the delay of my receiving the expected offer to work at AMC.

Having saved their butt on the Ram Truck intermediate shaft issue, I was ready to teach them how to design a chassis right. Little did I know, rather than me being the teacher, I was the student. Those that I worked with in the design department considered me a traitor, as we had regarded AVP as the enemy. I thought I would be helping them out by getting a better design done in AVP before they got it.

When I hired in at GM with TSI, some of my peers asked about my career goals. I expressed then I wanted to work on "Concept Cars." Be on the leading edge of what's new in the Industry. They said only the smartest got to do that. "That's right." I replied with my youthful arrogance. Chrysler's research arm was Liberty, but Liberty was still out of reach for me. AVP was the next best thing; the only work done was on future products. It was one step closer to the pure research I wanted to do.

Part 3

JEEPS

Chapter 11

ADVANCED VEHICLE PACKAGING (AVP)

New Jeep

The AVP department was divided into two groups, Dodge Trucks and Jeeps. I was in the Jeep group. The Grand Cherokee had been handed off to the design departments and the next project was to renew the Jeep Wrangler, the icon of the Jeep brand. The word "Jeep" is the second most recognized word in the world. The first word is "Coke." Renewing the Wrangler required us to preserve the Jeep image. When I worked in the design department, I had the occasion to read a book titled, The 50 Year History of Jeep. In my opinion, Jeep had survived due to a successful design philosophy. Shortly after WWII, Jeep had established a philosophy which has carried it for many years since. Jeep did not have the resources to redesign their vehicles every few years; thus they determined to create Jeep designs that would remain current for many years. The CJ line started in 1953 and continued until 1985, the Jeep Station Wagon and pickup 1948 to 1961, the Wagoneer line from 1962 to 1988, Cherokee from 1984 to 2001 and Wrangler 1986 to 1995. There were some failures along the way, two attempts at Jeepsters and the FC truck line for example, among others.

Jeep had two letter codes for its various models. Most may already know that CJ stands for "Civilian Jeep". SJ stood for "Senior Jeep" which was the old full size Grand Wagoneer and full size truck. XJ was the Cherokee, YJ the Wrangler, ZJ the Grand Cherokee. The 1997 newly redesigned Wrangler was the TJ which stood for "Tough Jeep." The KJ is the new Jeep Liberty. The XYZ codes had no meaning that I knew of. I think KJ stood for "Knew Jeep," meaning a new Jeep.

"60 Minutes" exposed the CJ's tendency to roll over when its' drivers had been drinking. This resulted in the design of the YJ Wrangler which was a redesign of the CJ. With the Wrangler, it was difficult to get one to roll over even when you were drunk. The redesign of the CJ to make it a Wrangler involved the addition of a "track bar" or panhard rod to the suspension. This was effective at preventing the Wrangler from rolling over in nearly all conditions. The down side is that it bound the suspension up, so the ride quality was very poor. In addition, because of the bound up suspension, stiffer springs were required to meet durability requirements, making the ride even worse.

Some cosmetic changes were made to distinguish it from the CJ, most significantly the square headlights. When asked if they wanted a Jeep, most people would answer "yes", but not one with the square headlights. What they meant is they wanted a CJ.

Chrysler did a lot of consumer research on the Wrangler. This had a great influence on the design process that created its replacement. Some of the research is worthy of mention here. The research showed the reason most people bought a Wrangler was just because they had always wanted a Jeep. At the time my 9-year-old niece listed a Jeep as one of the things she wants in her life. She's part of a crowd. Research also revealed that rarely did anyone buy a second one. The biggest complaints about the Wrangler were the poor ride and the noise from the soft top. And customers always mentioned they liked the round headlights better.

At the time, I leased a Wrangler through the Company Lease Program. With its bound up suspension, I started regular visits to a Chiropractor. I also made the mistake of ordering it with the soft-top and had to wear ear-plugs to prevent losing my hearing. I sometimes hoped some other driver would swerve into me, so I would have to drive a loaner vehicle until it was repaired. It was no wonder no one ever bought a second one.

The CJ was known for it's off road capability. With lift kits, larger tires and drivetrain modifications, this capability could be greatly enhanced. This is the very reason for a Jeep. The Wrangler was lacking in this department. With its bound up suspension, its off-road capability was much less than a CJ. Even the lowly Cherokee was better off-road. The qualifying off-road test for a Jeep was the Rubicon trail in California near Lake Tahoe. Modifications were required for a Wrangler to easily traverse the trail. Chrysler had a press fleet of Wranglers in Reno that had been modified so they could easily cross the Rubicon trail with amateur drivers (flatlanders and the press). These modifications included the addition of a boiler plate skid plate and 31X10.50 tires. Hence the saying "Real Jeeps are built, not bought."

Jeep aficionados did not believe that AMC and now Chrysler really knew how to build a Jeep. "Real Jeeps" were CJs or Wranglers, with bigger tires, suspension and drivetrain modifications. On a Jeep test trip to Moab, Utah, a local explained it like this: "When I retired and moved to Moab, I had a car. There are many off-road trails that take you to some very beautiful places. This is why I moved to Moab, so I could get far away from crowds and be out in the beauty of God's creations. My car wouldn't go off-road; neighbors said I needed a truck. I got a truck and went to many more places than I had with the car. I learned about other places people went to. My truck would not go to some of these places. I was told I needed 4-wheel drive to reach many of them. I bought a Ford Explorer and went more places than I did with my truck. There were still some places I could not reach. To get to these places, neighbors told me I needed a Jeep. I was reluctant to buy a Jeep, but finally did and went to nearly every place I had heard about and found a few new places to go. Still a few obstacles stood in my way. I was told I needed to modify my Jeep to conquer these last obstacles. I finally built a 'Real Jeep' and could go anywhere there was a road!"

In Michigan, I met a lot of people who were "flatlanders." Growing up in the West, I did not know what a "flatlander" was. It is a "wimpy" mentality I define as; "I'm not going down a road until it is paved first." Often in the West, we go places no one else has gone before, kind of a pioneering spirit. On the few occasions I had been in a Jeep before moving to Michigan, we were using them to traverse very difficult roads. Until shortly after transferring to the AVP department, I did not have the opportunity of going on a trip across the Rubicon Trail. Those that had been, told stories of how phenomenally difficult the trail was. When I finally went, it just seemed pretty typical of what you do with a Jeep out West. Then it occurred to me that "flatlanders" were telling me how difficult it was. Most of the "press" is from the East; accordingly they are also "flatlanders."

On the trip out to the Rubicon, the Chrysler Western Regional Sales Manager made a request for the new Wrangler. When he learned my position, he asked me to see that the new Wrangler is offered with the 31X10.50 tires as an option. The optional tires currently available were not big enough for the typical Wrangler customer. Dealers were ordering the Wrangler with the base tires, because the tires would be thrown away. Then they installed big tires (bigger than offered by the factory) and put the cars in their showrooms. This was done at very little profit for the dealer. If Chrysler made these tires available from the factory, the dealers would make more money. So would Chrysler.

With all this information, goals for the yet undesignated TJ were established: CJ off-road capability, YJ Wrangler resistance to roll-over, Grand Cherokee ride quality, lowering soft top noise levels and round headlights, in addition to meeting all the new federal regulations. And we were given a budget of $125 million for the whole project. This is the capital budget for new tools and tool changes to manufacture the new vehicle. This is miniscule; a typical refresh for most vehicle lines will run closer to 10 times this amount. With the request for large tires and my western upbringing (pioneer spirit), I had a personal goal to end the reality of the saying that, "Real

Jeeps are built, not bought." This included offering the 31X10.50 tires. I was quite naive in this goal, as I was dealing with "flatlanders" in the Chrysler organization.

Our manager was Don Sanders. His engineering team included a few engineers with different specialties and a design supervisor. This time was the highlight of my career. Don trusted those that worked for him and empowered them. I can't say I ever got to know Don very well; nevertheless he was a pleasure to work for. The success of the '97 Wrangler (TJ) is a testament to his management skill. Perhaps with the exception of soft top wind noise, the goals for the TJ were met, but it was not easy. Many battles were fought on many fronts with competing departments. I failed to convince those who make the decision to offer the 31X10.50 tires to offer them, however I did get the sheet metal moved so they can be added to the vehicle without modification.

Unintended acceleration

Howard Lester is a Human Factors Engineer and was a part of Don's team. He was responsible for ergonomics in the vehicle. This is an oversimplification of what he does. More to the point, he makes sure the occupant of a vehicle is comfortable and can easily operate the vehicle. I learned a lot from Howard. I sat kitty-corner from him for most of my time in the department. He's probably the best in the business.

Howard had a thorough understanding of "unintended acceleration." "60 Minutes" annihilated Audi car sales with their exposé of this issue. Eventually, Audi was able to prove the drivers were pressing on the accelerator pedal and not the brake pedal. The same issue caused a little grief at Chrysler on the Grand Cherokee. However, with Howard's expertise on the issue, Chrysler did not fall victim to the same fate as Audi.

The real causes of the problem are in the design of these vehicles, human expectations and stupidity. The Audi, like the Grand Cherokee, is a vehicle with four-wheel-drive. To make room for the four-wheel-drive components, the pedals were positioned farther left from the driver than on non-four-wheel-drive vehicles. With the pedals positioned farther to the left, some people may mistakenly step on the gas pedal when they are trying to step on the brake pedal. Most people, when they mistakenly step on the accelerator because it is where they expect the brake to be; notice the vehicle accelerate and release the pedal and step further left to find the brake. Occasionally, a really stupid person gets in the vehicle. When they accidentally step on the accelerator because they think it's where the brake should be and notice the vehicle accelerate; this stupid person still thinks they have stepped on the brake and pushes the pedal harder. This is unintended acceleration. In today's society, it is the manufacturer's responsibility to protect people from their own stupidity. Thus the natural selection process has been thwarted and our society grows stupider. Craig Lynn, then the Chief Engineer for all of Jeep, took reporters for rides in the Grand Cherokee and demonstrated that the engine could not overpower the brakes, and the negative press never took hold.

Engineering gender

The world of engineering seems to be dominated by those of the male gender. But with the liberalization of women, more and more women were coming into the engineering world. It seems they always got into jobs where they were engineering "soft" things, such as seats, seatbelts, dashboards, carpet, colors, etc. The ladies left the design of the "hard" stuff like engines, transmissions, suspensions, etc to us men. True to this stereotype; a woman engineer joined our department to help Howard out with the design of seats.

Her name was Elizabeth Corrales. The name Corrales (this is an alias) is somewhat well-known at Chrysler as her father had been in engineering for many years. I suspect for this reason she didn't take her husband's name when she got married. The intent was that some of Howard's expertise could be passed on. She was well-dressed, quite attractive, and quite ambitious to the detriment of the goal of becoming a Howard clone. Looking out for her future, she left our department and took a job in Europe at a manufacturing plant. The job was very enhancing for her career. Her husband took a two-year leave of absence from his job and toured Europe. I was kind of jealous of him.

Bob Bachelor

Though I was supposed to replace Bob, I more or less became his apprentice. He stayed on after his third retirement as a consultant, though he began working a few less hours. They kept giving him interesting things to do (my jobs, but I got to help). Our executive at the time, Gerry McCarthy, had at one time worked under Bob, and had immense respect for his skills and knowledge, so I kind of had to work in Bob's shadow while I was in AVP. This was very rewarding and frustrating all at the same time. I learned more from Bob than anyone else I ever worked with. Even though I was quite influential in the design of the TJ, my influence was not visible to anyone but Bob. Nevertheless, the rewards outweighed the frustrations. I really enjoyed working with Bob and counted him as a friend.

With the prevalence of many engineers who were not so smart, Bob and I on occasion had conversations on what makes one engineer smarter than another. He said that for any product to be on the market, it must of course work. In his terms, "you must assume function." The engineer that can do it for less money is the smarter one! In other words, whoever does it for the cheapest is the smartest.

I am often approached by acquaintances wanting to talk cars. In these conversations they seem to be seeking validation that their vehicle purchase was the smartest. Such as, isn't Mercedes the best car, or aren't Ford Trucks the best, etc. Applying Bob's "Smarter Engineer" concept to their purchasing decision, if they got the best value for the function they desire, their purchase was the smartest. Mercedes clearly builds some of the finest automobiles in the world, but they don't do well driving off-road, so it wouldn't be smart for me to buy one. I would pay way too much when it doesn't even have the function I require. Image can also be a required function of a vehicle purchase; often it is the most significant. Bottom line is; if you are happy with your purchase, it was a smart decision. You all have your validation now!

Chapter 12

JEEP SUSPENSION DESIGNS

General Concepts

I assume many of you reading this have relatively little knowledge of vehicle suspensions. In this chapter, I will attempt to teach you a few basics about suspensions. I apologize in advance for this technical discussion. Just like front end alignment, this could be another bushel of pine cones being rammed up your nose.

A vehicle suspension's purpose is primarily to keep the tires in contact with the ground. Bumps sometimes will cause the tire to lose contact with the ground. When the tire is not in contact with the ground, bad things can happen. A good suspension prevents bad things.

Suspension designs fit into two categories, beam axle suspensions and independent suspensions.

Beam axle suspensions were originally used on wagons. Today they are still used on heavy trucks and on some light rear wheel drive vehicles. Equipped with leaf springs, this design is very cheap. Often on lighter weight vehicles, the ride quality can be quite poor (Wrangler as an example). To improve the ride quality, coil springs with a four or five bar linkage is used (such as on Cherokee and Grand Cherokee) with some added expense. The Jeep design is known internally as the Link/Coil suspension.

Independent suspensions usually use a coil or torsion spring (on rare occasions a leaf spring) with a-arms. They are more costly, but offer benefits over the beam axle designs. This design is used almost exclusively as the front suspension on light vehicles in many variations. It is also becoming more widely used on rear suspensions. For my discussion here, it is only important to understand there are the two categories of suspension types (beam axle and independent).

To describe the operation of a suspension, I must teach you some new words. These will make you sound real smart when talking to your mechanic. When the tire hits a bump and moves towards the vehicle, this is called jounce travel or "jounce." When the tire moves away from the vehicle, such as into a chuckhole, this is called rebound travel or "rebound." When the vehicle is parked and there has been no movement, the tire is considered to be at the "curb" position. The total amount the wheel can move through jounce and rebound is the "suspension travel".

The ability of the suspension to respond to the bump or chuckhole is the "frequency." A high frequency responds faster, and a low frequency responds slower. There is not an ideal "frequency." Lower frequencies provide for a smoother ride. Higher frequencies improve handling.

To understand "frequency", think of audio speakers: A woofer handles "low" frequencies. To create the bass sounds, large movements of the speaker cone is required. Big magnets energize to move the big cone. Because of its mass, the big cone cannot move quickly enough to create high frequency sounds. A tweeter does the high frequencies; small, lower mass parts move very quickly to create the highs. A tweeter does a poor job with low frequencies because it can only make small movements.

The same principles apply to vehicle suspensions. A high frequency suspension will move the tire quickly in reaction to small bumps in the road. On large bumps, it will move to the limit of its reaction and the driver will feel the bump. Similarly, a tweeter does not have enough movement to handle the large movements required to make low sounds. On a low frequency suspension, large bumps are easily absorbed, but the reaction is too slow to absorb the small bumps, and the tire will lose contact with the road. With contact to the road interrupted, handling is compromised. As with cheap audio speakers which compromise the highs and the lows, most automobile suspensions do the same. Very expensive "Active" suspensions do try to give you the benefit of both. Most often though, a very good compromise can be found, and an active suspension is not used.

The "spring rate" (force required to compress a spring a specific distance) affects the frequency. Other things also affect the frequency; the biggest factor beyond the spring rate is called the "unsprung mass". This is generally the mass of the objects between the spring and the road. Note that tires are also a mini-suspension in and of themselves (bless the invention of the pneumatic tire). They have an associated spring rate and frequency.

Advantages of beam axle designs

Most automotive types don't think there are any advantages to beam axle suspensions, except they are cheap to manufacture. They have higher unsprung mass, so high frequencies are more difficult to achieve. This can compromise handling because the tire may not stay in contact with the road. Mr. Bachelor taught me there were many advantages besides the low cost of manufacturing.

One advantage surprising to me is that of handling superiority. Bob argued a beam axle holds the tires more square to the road, consequently keeping more of the tire in contact with the road. As a consequence, better handling. This is true; assuming frequencies are equal, meaning the tire stays in contact with the road equally. Hence you would expect race cars to use beam axle designs. However, beam axles suspensions are never able to match the high frequencies of independent designs. On most race cars, this is more important than keeping the tire square to the road. Even race tracks have bumps; consequently a higher frequency is most important.

But Bob wasn't racing. On a Jeep suspension, lower frequencies are desired for a good ride and can be achieved with both designs. With frequencies matched, the beam axle has superior handling. The press always berated the Jeep Grand Cherokee for its antiquated suspension, and then praised its handling as superior to the competition with independent suspensions. Bob knew his stuff!

Off-road capability is generally superior with a beam axle design, as larger articulation travel is achieved. This provides greater ability to keep the tires in contact with the ground. A typical beam axle suspension (such as on a Grand Cherokee) will allow one tire to be in contact with the ground 12+" higher or lower than the other tire in contact with the ground. This is called articulation travel. To illustrate this, imagine driving onto a bump 12 inches high. One tire is on the 12 inch bump and the other three are touching the ground. In contrast, the Dodge Dakota with 4-wheel drive had an independent front suspension (IFS) with about 7" of travel. The Dakota could only drive up 7 inches of the 12 inch bump. Any higher and one of the other tires will come off the ground and it will lose traction. Usually an IFS will have much less wheel travel than a beam axle design. Thus off-road capability with independent designs is more limited.

Advantages of independent designs

Bob didn't think there were any advantages of an independent design, but there are a few. I already covered the benefits in race cars. The other significant advantage is the characteristic of the vehicle's directional stability. When one wheel encounters a bump, the suspension at that wheel manages the disturbance and does not affect the other wheels. The vehicle is more stable driving straight down a road.

These advantages are very significant and that is why most light passenger vehicles use independent front suspensions (IFS) and rear independent suspensions are rising in popularity. Despite the excellent characteristics of the Chrysler vehicles which use a front beam axle design, they all experienced serious customer satisfaction issues that related to directional stability (an example is the Cherokee problem I traveled to France to repair). Corrections to the problem would have been a simple adjustment with an IFS design. There is much more to suspension design than the background I have provided here, but this information should be sufficient for the next few stories.

Chapter 13

DESIGNING THE TJ

New suspension invention

Scattered among the engineers at Chrysler, there was a contingent that strongly believed the future for Jeep should be independent suspensions (or at least to modernize the Jeep into the '90s). There was another contingent (mostly executives with formal authority) who trusted Bob Bachelor. Bob reminded everyone of the advantages of the beam axle designs; most significantly off-road capability and lower cost. In the end, Bob's influence prevailed and the new TJ was designed with a beam axle design almost identical to that of the Grand Cherokee. Ultimately the decision was made on cost and not on off-road capability.

In order for an IFS design to have equal off-road capability, wheel travel must be increased by about 50 percent to about 12". The Hummer had the longest wheel travel on an independent design at the time with 8". The challenge in achieving this much wheel travel in an independent design is the universal joint angle design limits in the drive shafts. Off-road racecars use very exotic joints and achieve large amounts of travel, but do not put torque through these joints except when necessary. The joints will fail quickly if constantly subjected to torque. This design is not acceptable for a consumer vehicle.

We invented an IFS design which did not compromise the drive shaft angles and had 12" of travel. This design had off-road capability equal to the beam axle design. It did increase unsprung mass about 25 percent vs. a shorter travel IFS. Although it still had lower unsprung mass than a beam axle design. The cost to manufacture this suspension was about that of the Dakota IFS at the time. The Dakota IFS cost more than double the cost of the Grand Cherokee front suspension. In fact a corporate bean counter aware of this, suggested using the Jeep front suspension on the Dakota as a cost cutting measure. The idea was rejected; most thought eventually Jeeps would have the more expensive suspension too.

The creative force behind the new Long Travel IFS was an old designer, Gerry Hennesy. Gerry had been around as long as Bob. I have often heard a common myth that it takes fresh young minds to invent new technology.

"They haven't gotten in a rut with their experience and are able to 'think outside the box.'" Gerry made this a myth. He was an old guy that was more creative than any young whippersnapper I ever met. And he did all this on paper. When they made him learn the computer, he decided to retire. What a great loss! If Gerry had a weakness, it was that he always thought if he could do it again; he could do the job better. Subsequently he never thought he was done with any job. I assisted him in solving some of the problems with his original concept for the Long Travel IFS. He was not interested in doing the gyrations to get it patented, so I did the gyrations and both our names are on the patent.

Hearing many stories about Gerry at his retirement party, I suspect he invented many things he never got credit for. The modern CV joint that makes front wheel drive cars viable was possibly the result of Gerry. The inventor that claims credit, worked closely with Gerry back in the '50s. With my experience with Gerry, it would not be hard to imagine he came up with the concept but never got credit for it.

Once a vehicle is designed, prototypes are built and tested and evaluated to determine if the objectives are achieved. Further design changes usually result. Glaring errors in the designs are exposed and other ways to improve the design are usually discovered as the prototypes are tested.

The group of engineers that do this work is the Vehicle Development department. A subgroup in this department which I mention again is the Vehicle Dynamics department. Their significant contribution is they do the fine-tuning of the springs and shock absorbers (also known as the "tuned assholes"). As is typical with most engineers, the Vehicle Dynamics engineers think they are the smartest and the most important. Most of them were wannabe racecar drivers (a truly talented racer wouldn't be holed up in a cubicle at Chrysler). The lot of them thought of themselves as "purists" and they lobbied for an IFS for the TJ. When we showed them Gerry's IFS, they viewed the increase in unsprung mass as spoiling the "purity" of an IFS, and would not support the design.

However with the ride quality goals of the program, this "compromised design" would have easily achieved the program goals. Yet the biggest reason it never got any traction was because Gerry and I came up with it. We had no "Formal Authority." One designer became an avid supporter of the design, Bob Sheaves, but again he possessed less "formal authority" than Gerry and I. Bob Bachelor (who possessed an immense amount of "informal authority" with those who had "formal authority") correctly pointed out its higher cost and only comparable off-road performance.

Not invented here

You may have seen a recent commercial on TV of a boss having a meeting: One of the employees makes a suggestion and the people around the table remain silent. Then the boss makes the same exact suggestion and everyone cheers. In this case, because the boss could take credit for thinking it up, it was rightly adopted. However, most people with such authority will reject any idea just because it was not their idea. This is what I call the "Not Invented Here" syndrome.

I would have expected the Vehicle Dynamics department to be supportive of the long travel IFS which Gerry had invented. It gave them what they asked for, the benefits of an IFS, without compromising on the benefits of the beam axle suspension. However with the debacle of the Jeep Cherokee steering pull issue, the *Go-Cart* (Vehicle Dynamics executive) despised me. And any idea which looked at all related to having anything to do with me was pooh-poohed. So the innovative suspension fell victim to the "not invented here" syndrome. Probably many innovations suffer the same fate. Imagine how much better cars could be today if the syndrome did not exist. This is a reason to get some "formal authority!"

Kinetic suspension

Even though you would think new innovations would come out of the Chrysler research department called Liberty or from AVP, most often the new innovations which had an impact on the products came from the design groups (if *they* thought of it, it didn't fall victim to the "not invented here" syndrome). One such innovation which the design groups were pursuing at the time was known as the Kinetic suspension system.

There were some engineers down under in Australia which invented the system and they were trying to get Chrysler to buy the patent rights. Chrysler eventually purchased the patent rights, because we outbid Mercedes-Benz. And history proves that this was a brilliant move! Maybe this was the reason for the merger with Daimler? The prime promoter of the system inside Chrysler was not even a Chrysler employee, but a contract engineer, Dave *Payemore*. His antics drove the price to over $30 million.

Dave was one of these people that became an engineer with on the job experience (he was glad to oblige some empire building manager way back). He had no degree and therefore was never a direct hire. But with 30 years experience he had gained some skills and no longer was his résumé fraudulent.

The system used essentially two gas strut springs at each wheel that were interconnected to the other wheels to always keep the vehicle level. This had significant advantages in that it acted similar to an active suspension system. This greatly improved off-road capability as ground pressure at each tire could be more consistently maintained. Later the name of the suspension was changed to the Overland suspension. But I have yet to see it come into production.

Building prototypes

When experimental systems are prototyped (such as a suspension system); they are usually adapted to a current vehicle. These types of prototype vehicles are called "mules". We thought it appropriate to build two mules: one with the Grand Cherokee type suspension front and rear, the other with the Long Travel IFS and a Grand Cherokee type rear suspension. This required the use of skilled fabricators. Often this work is farmed out to outside contract shops, or is done by our internal lab staff. We were told we did not have the budget to farm it out, and internal priorities did not allow our staff to do the work. We did get the mules built nevertheless.

We found some Union help at the Toledo assembly plant that were skilled craftsmen. Skilled fabrication work at the assembly plants was normally farmed out to save money. So to keep these skilled union people employed, they were kept on to sweep floors. This makes sense to me (not!). They volunteered to build our mules (this was more interesting than sweeping floors). I spent several weeks commuting regularly to Toledo to supervise the building of these mules.

Some of the parts we used on the mules were current production parts used on the Dodge vans built across the river in Canada. To order the parts through normal channels and to get them through Customs was about a 2-week project. I was quite familiar with the van assembly plant (I'd spent a lot of time there earlier in my career). So I drove over to the plant with my briefcase. Then I asked to see someone I knew and left my briefcase at their desk (they weren't there). Then I walked out into the plant and picked the parts I needed, took them back and stuck them in my briefcase. I then drove back across the border. We got the parts on time and I became a parts smuggler.

In our rush to get the mules built quickly, we had neglected to design an anti-sway bar. So for the mules we placed it on top of the frame in front of the grill, thinking a better design would be done later. A better design was never found and today the TJ has the sway bar under a fancy plastic cover in front of the grill on top of the frame.

Testing the mules

After the mules were completed, both were driven on local roads and some off-road testing was done. As Bob Bachelor predicted, the performance of both mules was very comparable. Thus the Grand Cherokee type suspension was selected for the new TJ. It was lower cost and performance on and off-road was not compromised. It made sense, but my instincts still favored the long travel IFS. It would offer better directional stability. A second mule with some improvements to the Grand Cherokee type design was built and delivered to Vehicle Development.

The Vehicle Dynamics engineer with the "tuned asshole" on the project was Steve Dunham. Steve had told us the suspension frequency which he desired, and as design engineers, we designed a spring which delivered on this frequency. We ordered this spring and iterations of springs stiffer and softer. I suppose Steve doubted his ability (actually doubting ours) to select the right spring, so he saved our spring recommendation for last. If I were in charge of development, I would test the recommended springs first and then test other iterations to make sure nothing works better. Another illustration of the "not invented here" syndrome. Steve didn't want us to be right and tested all the other springs first. Ultimately he selected the springs we had recommended. Steve didn't have such a big ego that he would let the syndrome prevent him from doing his best.

The Wrangler's stiff bound up suspension kept it from rolling over. In addition, it provided for excellent handling ability on pavement. With the new suspension for the TJ, the ride and off-road capability were significantly improved. With these improvements however, the handling ability on pavement was not to the level of the Wrangler. Steve deemed this as a compromise he was unwilling to make and threw a tantrum. He threatened to not do any tuning on the new suspension. He would recommend we just keep the old Wrangler design. In the end though, he found the new design acceptable and did a fine job of tuning it. Even though I called Steve a "tuned asshole", I would want him tuning a suspension on any car I would drive.

Definition of a Jeep

In order for a vehicle to wear the Jeep badge, it must first successfully cross the Rubicon Trail. The TJ suspension mule was shipped West and went over the trail easily and thus was deemed worthy to wear the Jeep badge.

Not all Jeep projects have met with the same success. Some years ago, a mini Jeep project internally known as JJ (Junior Jeep) produced some prototypes. When these prototypes were put to the test on the Rubicon, they did make it to the end, to the glee of Francois Castaing (VP of Engineering, the JJ was his idea). However it required much assistance with the help of a tow strap. Fortunately the project didn't go much further. The JJ was one of those programs that got cancelled in AVP. Thank goodness.

Though the long travel IFS was not selected for the TJ, a few of us thought perhaps it could have application on a future Jeep product such as the ZJ (Grand Cherokee). We wanted to take the TJ mule with the IFS across the Rubicon. Executives at the time would not approve the testing of the IFS mule on the Rubicon Trail; fearing exposure on the trail could lead to publicity about the design that could have a negative impact on the corporation.

They did allow us to take it to Moab, Utah for some serious off road testing. The trip though allowed, was largely unsupported. The corporation did ship the vehicle to the Arizona Proving Ground. I took a vacation to Arizona, picked up the vehicle, and drove it to Moab. Two of the designers who assisted in the design of the mule also took vacation and drove from Michigan to Moab. A few locals in the area volunteered to be our guides when we told them our purpose there. That was our test team and support. The first day we drove it up the Moab Rim trail. Other than a radiator problem we quickly repaired, the IFS mule had no trouble and was worthy to be a Jeep.

Moab trails have a different character than the Rubicon. You often look out your door and you are staring down several hundred feet. This can be quite disconcerting for a flatlander, needless to say the two designers stayed in their motel rooms after the first day.

Big tires

As previously mentioned, it was my personal goal to end the reality of the saying, "Real Jeeps are built, not bought." To meet this objective, the new TJ would need to be offered with the 31X10.50 tires. The largest tire available with the current Wrangler was a weird size; 29X9.50 or a P225/75R15. The base tire was a tiny P205/75R15. We determined that to fit the 31X10.50 tire into the new TJ; the front fenders needed to be moved 15 mm up from the road and some additional clearance was needed at the rear wheel openings. The feasibility of making these changes to the body was studied and seemed simple to do. We proposed these changes be made to accommodate the new 31" tires.

We were dumbfounded when the styling department chief, *Clever Tweed* rejected this proposal. Usually the styling department also pushes for the offering of larger tires and program management nixes it. Here program management asked for it and styling killed it. The argument went that most Wrangler's were sold with the base tires; and the TJ would look stupid with the base tires if it was designed to accommodate the 31" tires.

The problem with this reasoning is that most Wrangler buyers wanted 31" tires. Since they were not available; customers ordered the cheapest tires and then upgraded in the aftermarket. (Giving credence to the saying, "Real Jeeps are built, not bought"). These "customers" included our dealers. I was unsuccessful with this argument and no plans for the 31" tire were made. I didn't give up though; just a new strategy was employed.

In the design of vehicles, it was Chrysler's policy to provide ample clearance for snow chains on the base tire. Chrysler's clearance standard at the time was rarely adhered to, since it was a bit excessive. It was strictly adhered to on the Dodge RAM trucks; as a result, they did look stupid with the base tire. But not many RAM trucks are sold with the base tire (the same would be true for the new TJ if sufficiently large tires were offered). Most often, optional big tires are installed at the factory.

Funny thing: To provide ample tire chain clearance on the TJ, the front fenders needed to be moved 15 mm up from the road along with some additional clearance at the rear wheel openings. Thus the changes to the body sheet metal were made by strictly adhering to the tire chain clearance standard; but not to provide clearance for 31" tires. The chief designer *Clever Tweed* was very suspicious since the modifications were the same as previously requested. Not to be out maneuvered, the styling department designed the fender flares to not allow the fit of 31" tires. The premium tire on the TJ became a 30X9.50. If you install 31" tires, they don't hit any sheet metal; however, they can rub on the plastic fender flares. Later when I allowed compromise to the tire chain clearance standard on the '98 Cherokee, styling personnel accused me of providing clearance for 31" tires on the TJ. Guilty as charged!

Recently Jeep introduced the Rubicon edition of the Wrangler. It comes with 31" tires and a lot of other features that are normally added after you buy a Jeep to build one. Maybe you can buy a real one now! This model is selling twice as fast as they had planned. Dumb flatlanders! What thanks do I get?

TJ intermediate shaft

Remember back when I was the intermediate shaft expert, before I joined the AVP department. They did that dumb design where they had a suspension spring between the steering column and the steering gear. I did a dumb design which had three u-joints and a support bearing to snake around the spring. Remember that?

The majority of the design work on the TJ was done with the 4.0 liter engine. It was assumed to be the worst case design scenario as the 2.5 liter four cylinder engine was smaller. Early in my career with AMC I had done a preliminary design for the MPI intake manifold for the 2.5-liter. Later when MPI was adopted on this engine, the design didn't change much. This manifold was between the steering column and the steering gear. The dumb design I came up with that bent around things like this was used on the TJ. When the design was originally used on a Dodge Pickup suspension prototype, I thought it was ridiculous. Now it was the solution on the TJ. I should have patented it, but I thought it was a stupid design when I first did it. Later in the book I discuss stupid designs and patents. I didn't know this stuff about patents at the time and neglected to do it again.

Virtual reality

As with all my previous positions at Chrysler, I had a habit of getting so much done that my work got slow. The chassis design for the TJ was established, and the designs were given to the design engineering groups to be prepared for production. Our next project, the renewal of the Grand Cherokee for 1999, had not heated up yet. In the building of the mules for the TJ, there had been several glitches where parts did not fit according to the designs. This bothered me as adequate answers as to why were not available. So I took the opportunity while work had slowed down to get trained on CATIA myself. With my new skills on CATIA, I soon found the errors in sloppy mistakes which the designers had made in the "tube".

Additionally, I designed the TJ's inner wheel house. This is the big piece of sheet metal between the tire and the engine compartment. I dabbled in body design a little bit with this project. This was fun.

There was a company at this time that introduced an enhancement for CATIA called CATDADS. This allowed for analysis of dynamic systems in CATIA such as springs and bushings. I thought this would be a valuable tool in the design of suspension systems. However it still had bugs to work out and could not do the complicated problems I attempted with it. After doing a demonstration of it's capabilities at a trade show; I gave up on it. Perhaps when the bugs get worked out and with the more powerful computers nowadays, it might be useful. This was another attempt at my vision of a time when we could build virtual cars in the computer and virtually test them before building any hardware. The day may come. This experiment brought us a little closer.

Chapter 14

NEXT PROJECT

Grand Cherokee renewal

Working on the TJ program was perhaps the most rewarding time in my career. My supervisor Don Sanders had done such a fine job, that he was promoted and assigned to a new department. His replacement was the *Dick*. Obviously Mr. *Dick* was not of the same capability as Mr. Sanders, and he wasn't as much fun to work for. However, this change opened new doors for my career.

With our work on the TJ completed, our next project was the renewal of the Grand Cherokee or ZJ for the 1999 model year. The Grand Cherokee was a very successful product for Chrysler. There were some obvious reasons for this and some not so obvious. One of the obvious reasons was the Grand Cherokee's performance. The Grand Cherokee was manufactured with what in the industry is called uni-body construction. This makes for the body and chassis to be much lighter. So even with its old-style engines, it still outperformed the competition because it was 300 to 500 pounds lighter. Most of the competition used what is called body-on-frame construction; which is much heavier.

On this project, I had the privilege to go on some of the marketing research trips to assist program management. With my western sense of adventure, I chose two eastern cities where I hadn't been before; Atlanta and Boston. We interviewed people who owned the Grand Cherokee and some who owned its competitors. Grand Cherokee owners' biggest and almost only complaint was the spare tire location in the luggage compartment. Though owners of Grand Cherokees and competitors seem pleased with their purchase; the owners of the Grand Cherokees seemed more enthusiastic. One Grand Cherokee owner in Boston particularly made an impression on me: he mentioned he had owned many cars in his life and the Grand Cherokee was the one he liked to drive the most. He pointed to a late-model BMW in the parking lot and said, "I'd like that car in my garage. Will you drive it home for me? I'll drive my Grand Cherokee."

Since the owner seemed typical, and was more articulate than most, we diligently questioned him as to why he loved his Grand Cherokee so much. He said it didn't make him tired when he drove it. When he drove his Mercedes for several hours, he felt he had to take a nap. But after driving his Grand Cherokee for several hours, he felt refreshed. The Grand Cherokee had been one of Chrysler's most successful products at the time, and it was a prime goal of the Corporation not to screw it up. I felt a complete understanding of why this customer loved the Grand Cherokee so much would help us achieve this goal.

I queried Howard Lester, the human factors expert, about what would cause this phenomenon. He mentioned what makes a person tired is when the blood in their limbs does not circulate. People need to "fidget," as he termed it, to circulate their blood. He said for a seat to be comfortable, it has to have three or more comfortable positions for a person. If not, they can't fidget and will grow tired quickly. Through our brainstorming on this issue, we came to the conclusion something in the design of the Grand Cherokee was assisting in the circulation of the occupant's blood to their limbs.

The thing unique to the Grand Cherokee was the Link/Coil suspension. Both Bob Bachelor and I had driven Dodge Dakota pickups for two years (IFS suspension) and then switched to Jeep Cherokees (Link/Coil suspension). Both Bob and I made frequent trips to Northern Michigan. This owners experience prompted us to think about our own experiences. Both Bob and I noted when we drove the Dakotas, we had to stop and get refreshed frequently. But with our Jeep Cherokees we rarely stopped to rest. We had found another advantage of the cheap Jeep suspension. We concluded it was the suspension frequency of vibration that contributed to the circulation of the driver's blood.

Reliability vs. Durability

Another significant advantage of the Grand Cherokee was the range. The Grand Cherokee could be driven about 300 miles between gas tank fillups. Most competitors could only do about 200 miles. The Grand Cherokee had a 23 gallon fuel tank, while the competitors had smaller tanks, 18 to 20 gallons. Thus visits to the gas station are less frequent with a Grand Cherokee.

Why is this an advantage? Chrysler had a policy of continuing education. Often these classes we took were of little benefit, filled with a bunch of politically correct crap. Nevertheless one class which I attended some years back made an impression on me. In the class reliability was explained. **"<u>Reliability</u> is the ability of a product to perform its intended function without interruption."** They defined "interruptions" as anything that prevents the product from doing what it is designed to do. An automobile is designed to move the driver and occupants to their desired destination. If you stop to fill the gas tank, this intended function is interrupted.

Filling the gas tank, like changing the oil, are necessary for the vehicle to perform its intended function. These are called "planned interruptions." Planned interruptions are necessary. Other planned interruptions are; rotating tires, tune-ups, etc. Some interruptions are more severe than others. A tune-up is more severe than filling the gas tank. The other type of interruption is called "unplanned." This is when a component of the vehicle fails and needs repair. Examples of these are a flat tire, overheating, dead battery, transmission going out, etc. The transmission going out is more severe than a flat tire. A "more reliable" vehicle is the one with the fewest and least severe "interruptions." We do not distinguish between planned or unplanned interruptions in making this reliability judgment.

"Durability" is defined as the ability of a product to not need repair. In terms of reliability, it is the lack of frequency and severity of only the "unplanned interruptions." I don't think very many people understood reliability, certainly J.D. Power did not. The J.D. Power measurement of conditions per 100 vehicles was a measure of durability, not reliability. With the Grand Cherokee's long range, stops at the gas station were less frequent, so the frequency of all interruptions was best (or fewest) in class, making it the most reliable. I believe this a large factor as to why Grand Cherokee owners were so enthusiastic.

Comparing the Grand Cherokee to the Chevrolet S-10 Blazer, the Blazer had an 18 gallon fuel tank, but the spare tire is mounted under the cargo compartment! If you were to drive both for 12000 miles in the year, the Grand Cherokee would require 40 stops to fill the gas tank while the Blazer requires 53 stops. This assumes you fill the tank with three gallons left. All other things being equal and 10 minutes for each gas tank fill, the Blazer requires interruptions of an extra two hours each year. This may not seem significant, but any time in the busy world today is a bonus. And since the Grand Cherokee was best in class in this respect, it was another quality which endeared it to its owners.

Thus in my area of responsibility, I determined we needed to preserve the Grand Cherokee ride and the range. I received no argument in keeping the Grand Cherokee suspension with some improvements from those in authority. It was still the cheapest suspension to manufacture. But those I worked for determined; it was more important to move the spare tire out of the luggage space than to keep a large fuel tank. I was not successful at keeping a large fuel tank in the Grand Cherokee.

Another problem

At the time, the Grand Cherokee had been out for just a couple of years and its success was phenomenal. However, a few were being bought back. As I have previously discussed, a "buy back" occurs when the corporation (dealers and service engineering) are not able to correct a problem. It had to do with the fact the vehicle seemed to steer to the left while braking fairly aggressively. Internally the problem was labeled; "lead left while braking." No one understood why this was happening. A task force with engineers from Vehicle Dynamics, Product Engineering and Service Engineering was formed to address the problem. I was also asked to be a part of the task force as I was recognized as a steering expert. From Vehicle Development we had *Ever Workingonit* (remember him with the Cherokees pulling to the right) and Dave *Payemore* (he had been instrumental in driving up the price for the Kinetic suspension patent rights). Dave could drive any Grand Cherokee and later Cherokee and get it to steer to the left while braking.

Ever got me looking in the right direction (hey, I give credit where due), and I quickly understood why this was happening. Under a braking event, the rubber bushings in the control arms would change shape and the axle would "wind up" slightly. Because this was a beam axle suspension design, the winding up of the axle would result in slightly turning the tires to the left. This is one disadvantage of a beam axle suspension design. An independent design which is symmetrical will steer both wheels opposite and equal in a braking event. The Cherokee had the same suspension design as the Grand Cherokee. Why was it not an issue on it? Dave drove the Cherokees, and they did it too. I suppose Grand Cherokee owners are more discriminating. Although on the Grand Cherokee it was more severe as the control arm bushings were softer than the Cherokee's. The softer bushings helped the Grand Cherokee have a better ride.

How did we fix this? Well, we never really did. The fix is to go to an independent suspension. This requires a vehicle redesign; several years away. We could do things to reduce the severity: harder bushings in the control arms and improved steering linkage geometry. A new steering linkage also required a redesign of the vehicle. Because the Grand Cherokee was praised for its best in class ride, harder bushings were nixed. Ultimately we did nothing until the '99 Grand Cherokee. My recommendation to the Chassis Engineering Executive was to buy the vehicles back and sell them to other customers that would ignore the annoyance and enjoy the many other advantages of a Grand Cherokee. The corporation bought back less than 10 if my memory serves me correct. The Grand Cherokee was a very good vehicle. If you used your steering wheel, you never noticed this quirk. *Ever Workingonit* parked his instrumented Cherokee (he was still solving steering pull to the right), and every time you went to the proving ground, you now saw him in an instrumented Grand Cherokee, doing frequent stops. No one liked my answer, however no other answer was ever found.

As Bob Bachelor had taught me, the Jeep Link/Coil suspension had many advantages: it was cheap, best off road capability, excellent handling, great ride and frequencies that kept you refreshed while driving. On the other hand it lacked symmetry in its design and therefore had poor directional stability. This resulted in the steering pull problem on the Cherokee and the "lead left while braking" problem on the Grand Cherokee. The same suspension design was also utilized on the 4-wheel drive Ram trucks and of course the TJ. It wasn't long until *Ever Workingonit* had these vehicles instrumented also and he was driving them around the proving grounds too. I noticed on the new Jeep Liberty they have gone to a symmetrical IFS. It probably lacks in off road capability, but has excellent directional stability.

Big SUV

Also at the time, Chrysler was exploring the feasibility of doing a Sport Utility based off the Dodge Ram Truck. This was a great looking SUV. If Chrysler had proceeded with this vehicle, it would have been a hit. The Chrysler eggheads figured this segment of the market would not grow much and Chrysler would lose money in this market. Too bad, it would have looked great on the road.

Chapter 15

THE BEGINNING OF THE END

Newer boss

My new manager on the Grand Cherokee was Mr. *Dick*. He had made his mark by his involvement in managing a charity program at JTE. I used to think what was important to the Corporation was to get your job done and do it well. But, in the new age thinking of the '90s, it became more important how you made those you work with "feel." Job expertise became just a very minor part of the performance review process. This did not bode well for me. When I had to work with idiots, I had a difficult time not making them feel like the idiots they were. It was one of my few talents. Mr. *Dick* unfortunately was an idiot. However, he made everyone feel quite smart. You always feel quite dry when you observe someone who has fallen in a swimming pool.

These new politically correct corporate relationships seemed to start infecting Chrysler shortly after the merger. To get in touch with our customers, we went on trips to visit some of our dealers. The only thing I remember learning from my trip was the Jeep dealer wanted us to raise the price on the Jeep Grand Wagoneer (SJ). They were losing sales to the Range Rover just because it was priced higher (more about this phenomenon to come). Chrysler discontinued production of the SJ the following year.

I suppose this had been the beginning of the new management philosophies. We were to get in touch with our customers and make sure we always pleased them. Our customers weren't just the people who bought our cars; they were also people in the other departments we interacted with. AMC attitudes didn't worry about other people's feelings, but about getting the job done. This had prevailed for a time; although eventually the success this brought was overcome by the new "guides" on how to manage a big corporation.

Corrupt relationships

As we embarked on the redesign of the Grand Cherokee, Mr. *Dick* employed the new management philosophy where everyone was our customer and we were to make them happy. This new politically correct

87

management mumbo jumbo defined our customers as the Design and Vehicle Development departments. It was our job to please them. This was very contrary to what Bob Bachelor had taught me what our job was. Bob taught me, that when everyone was equally pissed off at us, then we had done a good job. I remember when I was in the Design department; I had been pissed off at Bob. Our department mediates between the various competing departments.

An example of this is on two areas of the Grand Cherokee that needed improvement; the brakes and the steering geometry (reducing the severity of "lead left while braking"). We determined to go to 16 inch wheels across the board to provide extra room for these improvements. The brake department submitted a proposal for the improvement with the larger wheels which left no room for improvements in the steering geometry. The suspension department submitted a proposal for improvements in the steering geometry which did not allow for any improvement in the brakes. The final design which we did had some improvement in both areas. But not to the extent either of the departments had requested. Both departments were pissed off at us. Both areas were improved!

The F1 Grand Cherokee

While we were starting on the design direction which kept the old suspension with minor improvements, we thought we should explore a more radical design. Of course the vehicle dynamics department wanted the new Grand Cherokee to have a four-wheel independent suspension. And my idiot boss wanted to please them because they were our customer. And they did not want us to design one with the long travel suspension we had invented on the TJ program. So they assigned their brilliant former Lotus employee pseudo engineer "*I-am Not-sharp*" to help us with the design and insure it was not our patented long travel design. Now, contrary to the opposite of his name, my opinion of *I-am Not-sharp* was that he was not too sharp. There was a reason he was no longer with Lotus.

At the time there was a shortage of designers in our department; because most were doing work on other projects. So to do the design on the four-wheel independent suspension Grand Cherokee, outside contract designers which were all from England were brought in. Designers from England were plentiful. The English auto industry had disappeared (due to "socialist" government policies over there, I might add) and there was an abundance of unemployed designers. Mr. *Dick* stripped me of my authority and *I-am Not-sharp* directed the design; he was English too. I was only supposed to assist *I-am Not-sharp* in the design of this proposal for the Grand Cherokee.

The design was ridiculous. It was a tubular frame (like a race car) with the engine placed at the center between the driver and the passenger. Of course it had a four-wheel independent suspension. It looked like a Formula One racecar with four wheel drive and five passengers seated uncomfortably. We had wasted six months and several hundred thousand dollars doing this foolish design.

The time came to show the design to upper management. Bernard Robertson was upper management (He was English too, but didn't join Chrysler because he was out of work, he was a bit sharper). I knew the design was stupid and told Mr. *Dick* so. I recommended we not show it to upper management, as it would bring embarrassment to Mr. *Dick* and our department. I was labeled negative and a troublemaker. I was right! It seemed that Bernard had difficulty not laughing at the proposal when it was shown to him, and I don't ever recall seeing Bernard laugh. Fortunately we had been working on the real design at the same time, and progress was being made on the Grand Cherokee program.

Idiot

Just like the *Juice's* underling being shoved aside with a research assignment; the example of *I-am Not-sharp* being assigned to work on this project and intruding into the business of our department is another illustration of an idiot being "shoved aside." His department wanted him out of their hair, so they gave him this "research" assignment with which he could delude himself was important. I made this observation and informed Mr. *Dick* of it on several occasions, but was ignored. On more than one occasion, I had gone into Mr. *Dick's* office and attempted to explain what an idiot *I-am Not-sharp* is. *I-am Not-sharp's* own department had shoved him aside with this project and it was a fantastic waste of time and company resources. In my frustration, my voice got loud and I called Mr. *Dick* an "idiot." Everyone in the surrounding offices and cubicles heard these confrontations.

With the Formula One Grand Cherokee project, I had failed in preventing my boss from looking like an idiot. I really missed Don Sanders. All the other geniuses which had worked for Don had gotten promoted and no longer worked for the *Dick*. Bob Bachelor now reported directly to the executive engineer, Gerry McCarthy. Bob had retired and was now on contract as a consultant. The others that had reported to Don had been promoted to specialists and also reported directly to the executive engineer. Of Don's original team, I alone still reported to the *Dick*, and he didn't like me (I suppose calling him an "idiot "in a loud voice didn't endear me to him). In the years I worked for Chrysler, my affection for the Jeep brand was strong, and I wanted to see the Grand Cherokee for '99 come to fruition. I was not looking to find another job; I figured I would just have to tolerate the idiot.

Golden opportunity

Once a year it's time for our performance review, usually in December. I usually did quite well on performance reviews, because I was quite competent and most knew it. However I didn't have high expectations with Mr. *Dick*. The process requires evaluating myself and then submitting it to my manager. On the last page of the review, there is a section where you list future positions/promotions with the Corporation that you are seeking. I didn't understand the need for "formal authority"; I had accomplished so much without it. I did not have a desire to be in management, but harbored my dream to do research. On the last page I had put one word, "Liberty".

As I have mentioned before, Liberty was the research and development group for Chrysler. They were located in Madison Heights. I had visited their facility on a few occasions, and was still under the belief that this is where Chrysler did their research. My most recent visit to their facility was to look at their electric car. The real Chrysler electric vehicle was not the Liberty design. A conversion of the Chrysler minivan held this mantle. Some of the early feasibility work on the electric minivan was done at Liberty. Then it was passed on to the minivan engineering group.

In addition to the performance review in which your manager evaluated and then shared with you, there was another performance review which evaluated you for your potential for promotion. It was in this performance review that future leaders of the Corporation were identified early in their careers. These leaders were identified as "high potential" long before they were promoted into management. Now I don't know this for sure, as I have never seen one of these reviews on anyone. Because the individual's review was never shared with that individual and I was never in management. My knowledge of the review comes from the fact the mature Mr. *Dick* bragged to me in one of my performance reviews he was looking at mine. He could make comments on it that would affect my career. In other words, I'd better suck up to him or he'll ruin me.

I had completed my self-evaluation and stopped by to drop it off on my way to the cafeteria for lunch. Mr. *Dick* was in at the time and quickly turned to the last page before I left his office. He excitedly asked if I was interested in working at Liberty. I said in the future I thought it would be interesting; however I desired to work on the Grand Cherokee for the next year or so. He said he was acquainted with someone who was an executive at Liberty, and asked if I would be interested in having him talk to this executive for me. I said I didn't care either way and went on my way to the cafeteria. I figured with his disgust for me, his talking to anyone wouldn't help my career.

I returned from the cafeteria some 15 minutes later and sat down at the computer to play some games while I ate my lunch. Before I finished my lunch, Mr. *Dick* came trotting back to my cubicle looking thrilled. He had talked to the executive at Liberty and they were looking to hire a chassis expert and I would be a good fit for the position. He encouraged me to submit my résumé and personal history for the position to personnel. I had the mistaken belief the '99 Grand Cherokee would get screwed up if I didn't stay in my position with the department. But Mr. *Dick* had the formal authority as my manager, and I transferred to Liberty in February of 1995. When they offered me an almost 12 percent increase in my salary, my affection for the Grand Cherokee waned and I took the new position at Liberty. I had gotten the "shove", Mr. *Dick* had given me a swift kick in the butt and I was gone.

Now it just occurred to me while writing this, that my view of the swift kick in my butt by Mr. *Dick* was just the ticket to my ultimate desire to do research for Chrysler at Liberty. Now I wish I had figured this out sooner. When you work in a large corporation that is afraid to fire anyone, **having a boss who doesn't like you is your best opportunity for promotion.** Perhaps I had misread Mr. *Dick*'s threat about the secret performance review; maybe he was telling me I could have anything I want, if I would just "please leave."

As discussed in an earlier chapter; my manager *Dave Drunk* benefited from this phenomenon. I speculated he had been an undesirable employee in his previous department. Therefore his previous manager gave him a glowing performance review and likely labeled him as "high potential" hoping another department would pick him up. He got picked up. And now that I think about it, we all had so much trouble with Mr. *Dick*, is it possible his previous department had trouble with him, and therefore he was brought into ours because he came so highly recommended. Dave's boss didn't like him, he got promoted. Mr. *Dick*'s boss didn't like him, he got promoted. My boss didn't like me, I got my dream job at Liberty. It seems the best opportunity for promotion is when you have a boss who doesn't like you.

Here's a new strategy: Call your boss an "idiot", so the whole department can hear. At the next performance review, ask for your dream job, and I'll bet you get it!

Part 4

DELUSION LAND

Chapter 16

LIBERTY

The Pontiff

Liberty had a strange organization. It was headed up by *"Dim Smore."* His grade level was general manager. He had three executive engineers reporting to him. I reported directly to one of these, Steve Spencer. The other two I will call *"Dim Wiser"* and *"Dee Lusion."* Then there were two layers of management missing. It was not a place with opportunities for promotion. It seemed that *Dim Smore* liked it that way, because he was the center of the universe with lots of authority and had the ability to make the minutest of decisions.

Dim Smore like many in Chrysler's upper management came over from Ford. After working in and observing the organization for over three years, I speculate he had not been selected to lead Liberty because of his competence. More likely, he had been "shoved" aside. Remember, Liberty was originally organized so Lee Iacocca would not be caught in a lie. Mr. *Smore* had a lot of degrees, but he was just an engineer. He was influential in helping me form my hypothesis about those with advanced degrees. When I originally interviewed for the position at Liberty, Mr. *Smore* was concerned about my lack of an advanced degree. I challenged him at the time; if after two months at Liberty, he could recall to bring it up, I would go back to school. This was my way of saying, "once you've seen my work, you won't find me lacking in competence."

Each year during the holiday season, *Dim Smore* would throw a Christmas party for the entire Liberty organization. To be politically correct; it was called a "holiday" party. It was usually fully catered at a very nice hotel, with a disc jockey and dancing for entertainment. *Dim* paid for the whole thing. My first cubicle at Liberty was next to an old retired engineer, *"Billy Cruiser."* I asked *Billy* if he were going. He said he wasn't, noting it was only another platform for *Dim Smore* to "pontificate" to the peasants. Pontificate was a new word to me, and I asked for an explanation. Then I went to the party and I really understood the meaning of the word.

Dim was from Texas (Texans are more blessed than people from

Michigan). He informed us if he had not become an engineer, he would have been one of the Oak Ridge Boys. As he told us, he sang with them in the church choir growing up in Texas. They went different ways when he left to become an engineer. They would have been even more successful if he had stayed with them. At the Christmas Party each year, it was our "privilege" to hear him sing with the Oak Ridge Boys. He "blessed" us with his voice harmonizing to a record he brought to the party (no one else was ever invited to sing, none of us were from Texas). We could hear how much better they would have sounded if *Dim* had been an Oak Ridge Boy too. The DJ would interrupt the dancing early, before anyone had a chance to leave, and put on the Oak Ridge Boys record. *Dim* harmonized as the song played. We all clapped for him: careful not to clap too much and prompt him to do another number. It reminded me of an old Andy Kaufman comedy sketch. But *Dim* seriously thought he was doing a great favor in singing for us half-assed karaoke style!

Misfit gathering

Liberty seemed to be a holding tank for the misfits of the corporation, yours truly included. All the decisions made at Liberty never had any effect on the products which we sold to the public. Remember the story of the *Juice's* underling that was assigned to do research. He deluded himself into thinking his research was very important; when in fact he was just shoved aside. At Liberty it wasn't just one individual, it was the whole organization. As in my case, when a manager or executive wanted to dispose of an undesirable employee, he told the employee about the opportunities at Liberty. It was much more difficult to fire someone, so instead they were shoved aside and sent to Liberty. Here they did "research" and they could think they were doing something very important. I almost got fired from Liberty, maybe because I wasn't delusional. Misfits come in all different stripes, the very competent who intimidated their bosses (as in my case), the incompetent and the zealots, etc. There were a few exceptions, like individuals that were brought on in an attempt to bring some credibility to the organization.

Here is an interesting misfit; one of my peers at Liberty was obviously very experienced and very competent. He did not hire into Chrysler until after his 40th birthday. The department he worked for in vehicle engineering had passed over him on several occasions for a promotion to manager. They opted for younger engineers who had been "raised" inside Chrysler (perhaps those labeled as "high potential" on their secret PR form). This employee thought this reeked of age discrimination and had brought a lawsuit against Chrysler. And soon after, the only position open to him was at Liberty. They could not fire him as that would be retaliation for his lawsuit and strengthen his position. However no one wanted him around because of the trouble this caused. Consequently he became one of the staff at Liberty; a misfit.

Respected executive

Steve Spencer's father was a longtime Auto Industry engineer who was quite well respected. At the time, pressure was brought by the Clinton/Gore administration for the automakers to develop better fuel economy cars in partnership with the U.S. government. Inside Chrysler, this task was given to Liberty. No executive on the Liberty staff at the time was qualified (nor respected) for this position. So Steve Spencer with his respectable name was brought on from another organization. He got a big promotion to head up Chrysler's "Hybrid Electric Vehicle" program. His official title was Chassis Executive Engineer. That is why I reported to him. Good thing too, because I couldn't have worked for the other two buffoons.

The three executive engineers had their design responsibilities divided into chassis, drivetrain, and body. *Dim Wiser* was over the design of the drivetrains, which included engines and transmissions. I don't think I ever saw him laugh or even crack a smile, except at the Christmas party when *Dim Smore* was singing. I never quite knew what to think of *Dim Wiser*, his talk seemed to make sense once in awhile, but his projects were always ridiculous.

Something like Enron

Recently I watched a made-for-TV movie about the Enron scandal. Enron reported profits on fraudulently optimistic projections of hoped for future sales (my interpretation from the movie). Accordingly investors and employees were bilked out of millions of dollars. At Liberty, we reported technological breakthroughs which had not occurred. I suppose this didn't bilk investors out of millions. It was more of a public relations effort. Hence Chrysler wasn't doing research; at least not at Liberty. It was just a bunch of pomp. Similar to a well known radio talk show host's description of liberals, the task at Liberty was, "How can we fool them today?" I eventually figured this out; that's why I decided to leave.

Chapter 17

CHEAP CAR

China Concept Vehicle

Dee Lusion was the body design executive engineer. Both *Dee* and *Dim Wiser* had a similar characteristic. They had egos as big as *Dim Smore's*. Everything they did or said was to demonstrate they were more important or superior than we who were not in their position. It was just like *Dim Smore*, but more obnoxious because they had less authority. Even though these executives had their responsibilities divided up among chassis, drive-train and body; most projects under their leadership included elements of all three. Each program was typically represented by a show car. Some of these would be shown to the public, others not. My first opportunity to demonstrate my competence came on a project which was under *Dee*.

Originally the project was known as the R2CV. R2CV is in reference to a "renewal" of the French people's car, the Citroen 2CV. It was assumed this would appeal to the engineering VP Francois Castaing. The idea was to build a very cheap car to sell in third world countries. However, more true to the Liberty method, it was a platform to demonstrate how smart Mr. *Smore* and Mr. *Lusion* were, or thought they were.

On the project, one goal was to mold the basic body out of plastic in three pieces, preferably from recycled pop bottles. It was similar to what is done on a simple toy car, but full scale. The vehicle was front wheel drive and used a Neon manual transmission attached to a 25 horsepower Kohler V-twin engine. Mr. *Lusion* had been impressed with the rubber suspension on an enclosed car-hauler trailer, so he and one of his cronies, *Billy Cruiser*, had adapted this type suspension to the car. A patent was applied for. The goal for the suspension was to have 10 inches of wheel travel. If my memory serves me correct, the car was to be manufactured for less than $1750. Eventually the target market for the program became China. Therefore the name was changed to the China Concept Vehicle (CCV).

The first prototype of the CCV was nearing completion when I arrived at Liberty. It had a double wishbone front suspension using rubber torsion springs. The rear suspension was a trailing arm design with rubber torsion springs. So it had a four-wheel-independent suspension (Thinking back on my suspension design discussion, not the cheapest design!). The front suspension design was incomplete, so I quickly finished the design to fit to the already fabricated frame. I actually worked some overtime in getting this part of the project done. The lab at Liberty was staffed by three union technicians. They did most of the fabrication of this prototype. Or I should say two of them did most of the fabrication, the other one was drunk most of the time. The molds to make the body had not yet been built. The prototype body was hand made fiberglass; supposedly to represent one molded from recycled pop bottles.

Union technicians

One of the technicians, Craig, was of exceptional skill and he was very dedicated. Often the engineers provided him inadequate information to properly fabricate the prototypes, so he had to do a lot of engineering on their behalf. He rarely got the credit he deserved. Bob was nearly as skilled as Craig, but not as dedicated. He never did more than you asked and he took his sweet time.

Bill, the 3rd technician was an example of why you don't want unions. He had been disciplined for drinking on the job on several occasions, but the union had made sure his employment continued. After I was first introduced to him, he always greeted me by calling me "Erv"; I suppose the name "Evan" was out of his experience. I felt sorry for him as he appeared to be of limited intelligence (having fried too many brain cells with booze), and I did not correct him on my name. This was a mistake. I had a fairly decent rapport with him, but he became the subject of ridicule behind his back for this error. After about two years, he finally figured out my name was Evan. That kind of shot the rapport.

Rubber suspension

The rubber suspension used on trailers had about ten times the spring rate (too stiff) required for this vehicle. The trailer suspension used a very short trailing arm. The spring rate could be softened simply by lengthening the trailing arm. This also increased the wheel travel to 10 inches in the case of the rear suspension. This seemed to be a very simple adaptation, so simple that one would wonder why it hadn't been tried before (actually it's been tried before). Perhaps Mr. *Lusion* was quite ingenious. Possibly this is the freethinking you get from someone who knows nothing about rubber and suspensions. I was initially in awe at the clever design this appeared to be. My knowledge in designing systems with rubber was limited and I could easily be snookered.

Mr. *Lusion* surrounded himself with similarly delusional people. *Billy*

Cruiser took on the role of development engineer with the CCV prototype. Once the suspension was done, I assisted him. He was an old guy with a lot of experience. Sometimes his age would show up and he acted a little senile. He had a really annoying quirk; he was a two-foot driver. He had his right foot on the gas and controlled the speed with his other foot on the brake. I tried to avoid riding anywhere with him because it was so annoying. Fortunately the CCV had a manual transmission, and it wasn't as annoying to ride with him in it.

The spring rates were about right and we were initially impressed with the performance of the suspension. We were testing at Chrysler's proving grounds in Chelsea, Michigan. Yet after the first few hours of testing, we noticed the vehicle body getting closer to the ground. Upon further investigation, we found the rubber springs had failed.

The rubber springs we used in the prototype were made by Goodyear. They had been obtained from a trailer parts supply house in the area. I contacted Goodyear and located an expert at designing rubber torsion springs. I became the student and soon learned how to design rubber springs. It was clear why the springs had failed. Lengthening the trailing arm dramatically increased the stress on the rubber. I came to a clear understanding of a principle in spring design; the lower the spring rate, the higher the stress in the spring material. On a trailer which carries a heavy load, a high spring rate is desired. Therefore rubber can be a good choice for a high rate spring on a trailer.

I searched patents on rubber suspensions. They are not a new invention. They have been in existence since the 1930s, mostly on large trucks, buses and trailers. Some had been tried on small cars; unsuccessfully because they had the same experience I was now having. On a small car, a low spring rate is desired. Rubber is not an intelligent choice, and every other carmaker seems to be intelligent as no lightweight vehicles utilize a rubber suspension.

I presented this information to Mr. *Lusion* and was surprised at his resistance to change the design. I did not yet understand his personal goal to have as many patents as possible demonstrated on this show car. For him, it was personal. I did however; design a spring in rubber to meet the requirements of the car. Each spring was about four times the size of the previous spring which failed. Also a suspension with this spring design was significantly more expensive to manufacture. The rubber rear suspension would cost about $120 per vehicle. Whereas with a simple suspension using springs made from steel would cost a little more than $50.

The front suspension could not meet the goal of 10 inches of wheel travel with the new rubber spring design. I designed an innovative suspension design which had 10 inches of travel, but it could not utilize the rubber spring. The rubber design was double the cost and could not meet the performance goals. What innovation!? A design with steel springs met the goals and was so much cheaper. Having made no progress with Mr. *Lusion*, I approached my boss with this dilemma. He was not successful with *Dee* either, and a meeting with Mr. *Smore* to settle the matter was scheduled.

I suppose to be a general manager; you must be somewhat politically savvy. The rear suspension with the redesigned rubber springs stayed. For the front, my new design with steel coil springs was selected.

A new patent

The management encouraged me to patent the new suspension. Shortly thereafter, some sketches related to the new suspension, showed up on my desk requesting that Mr. *Lusion*'s name also be added to the patent. My boss, Steve Spencer, didn't really believe that *Dee* had contributed on the patent. I rationalized it would more likely be issued with *Dee*'s name on it and didn't make any stink about it. After all, I was only interested in the patent award money. Having another name on the patent did not affect my bonus.

A problem

After building the second CCV prototype with the new suspension, a severe problem was discovered. I must introduce you to a new suspension design term, "brake anti-dive." When you apply the brakes of a vehicle, some of the weight from the rear of the vehicle is transferred to the front of the vehicle. The weight transference will cause the front suspension to compress or "dive". Suspensions are designed to have a characteristic which resists the dive, called "brake anti-dive." I only analyzed the suspension for this characteristic at the design or curb position. It had typical resistance to dive, which is only partial at this position. However as the suspension went into "jounce travel," with my new innovative design; resistance to dive disappeared. In fact it accelerated the dive. In plain English; if you stop the vehicle quickly, your front bumper would quickly go to the ground. This could cause a driver to lose control of the vehicle in certain conditions. It was not an acceptable design.

My accomplishments on the CCV were: I had designed an innovative front suspension that didn't work and a very expensive rear suspension with rubber springs. This was hardly a success in my eyes and nowhere near the goals for the project. Braking maneuvers were not a large part of the testing, so everyone was pleased with the performance of the suspension. I was embarrassed by it. I criticized it and lobbied to do a better design. No one wanted to here any criticism and my role began to diminish.

As far as handling was concerned, the suspension worked very well. On the test track at Auburn Hills, *Dim Smore* following in a minivan could not keep up with me in the little 25 hp CCV. On this and a few other occasions, he noted my excellent driving skills. He asked if I had been to Skip Barber's driving school. I had not. Chrysler in an attempt to get executives to learn to love driving sent them to race driving school. Some of us already had a love for driving, and already were skilled at it.

Illusions

It was the intent to injection mold the major body components, thus there would be no steel or frame in these parts of the body. There were concerns whether these components would have the strength to meet crash testing criteria. Consequently when a vehicle was prepared for the crash test, steel reinforcement beams were added to the plastic components. This was stupid. You wouldn't know if the plastic could pass the test! This totally invalidated the test; just another demonstration of the brilliant Liberty method ("How can we fool them today?") and a total waste of money.

Originally it was management's intent to develop the CCV for India, and a trip was made to meet with Indian officials. When interest in the car was not found in India, then a trip was made to China to see if the vehicle could be marketed there. China like India wanted a more sophisticated vehicle. Nevertheless the design direction did not change. They thought they knew better what the Chinese would want. And since this program was spending millions of research dollars, Chrysler executives didn't flinch. The illusion of research kept on.

Reinventing it

While visiting these other lands, *Dee* noticed how hot and humid it was in these other countries. He determined that a stand-alone air-conditioner that would work in the CCV would be a "cool" option for this program. You could also take it out of your car and use it to cool your house! Now Liberty had no air-conditioning experts on their staff. Yet true to the Liberty method, *Dee* had his staff design an air-conditioning module with a separate Briggs & Stratton engine to power it. It fit between the driver's and passenger's seat. I never remember them getting it to work. I did suggest that such things already existed for the cooling of refrigerated trucks. Maybe they could order one out of a catalog. Didn't matter, I was ignored and *Dee* got another patent.

Open minds

The manufacturing cost for the CCV program was way over budget. *Dee* approached me one day and asked what I could do to cut costs in the suspension. I told him I could save $70 in the rear suspension if I could use steel springs. He told me it had to be rubber. "You want a nickel or a dime?" I offered. *Dee* threatened, "I'll get another engineer that doesn't have such a closed mind to do it." I sarcastically begged, "Please!" He gave the design to another engineer, but the price didn't change much. I never worked on another *Dee* project again. My question is, "Who has the 'closed mind' when the only acceptable answer is rubber?" Delusional Dufus *Dee Lusion*!

There is a belief in engineering that everything can be improved upon. The belief gets corrupted by many. As with *Dee* and the rubber suspension illustrate: Because no one else does it, does not mean it is an improved system. Most often, the best design is the present one.

Chapter 18

INVENTIONS

Impressed?

I recently did a patent search at the government website. I am listed as an Inventor on eight patents. Up until now, I thought I only had seven. When I tell people that I have patents they are always very impressed. Sorry to burst everyone's bubbles. It's very easy to get a patent! The device or system does not have to work or even exist or make any sense. You can patent things that don't work; most patents are this type, several of mine included. You can even patent something that is already patented as long as you call it something different.

The patent office just issues the patents that are in the right format. To get a patent in the right format, you usually have to get a patent attorney to put it into words that no one can understand; then a patent will be issued. If you believe someone has infringed on your patent: the patent office doesn't do anything. Instead you hire an attorney and sue the violating party. A judge or a jury will decide if your patent has been infringed and what damages occurred. So if you have a truly innovative idea, it is important to patent it; so you will prevail in court. Additionally; when you patent something, the patent office publishes it so it becomes public domain. Everybody will know about it, and those that are creative will copy it and improve it before you can. Sometimes you may not want to patent it, so it will remain a secret.

This is a patent of *Dim Smore's* to illustrate some of these points. It is titled, *"Environmentally Sensitive Hybrid Vehicle."* The abstract reads:

"A hybrid vehicle includes a vehicle frame having a pair of rails disposed in spaced relationship relative to each other and defining a longitudinal axis of the vehicle, a pair of axles disposed spaced from one another and extending substantially transverse to the longitudinal axis with each of the pair of axles including a pair of wheels operatively mounted thereto for rolling engagement with a surface, an internal combustion engine mounted for driving engagement of one of the pair of wheels through one of the axles and an electric motor mounted for driving engagement of the other pair of wheels through the other axle, and a set of batteries disposed parallel to the longitudinal axis of the vehicle and between the internal combustion engine and the electric motor for providing an electrical power source to the electric motor."

I'll try to translate: A car with an engine to drive either the front or rear axle and an electric motor powered by batteries to drive the other axle. The benefit of such a hybrid vehicle is that a connection of the engine to the electric motor is not required; the road accomplishes this between the two axles. Now I will be straight with you and will compliment Mr. *Smore* on the ingenuity of using the road to connect the two power sources together. This also presents some other problems, but for this discussion we'll pretend they don't exist. Why the title "Environmentally Sensitive Hybrid Vehicle?" We are supposed to believe this hybrid is more sensitive to the environment than another one. It contains all the same parts as other hybrids, just in words no one understands. It doesn't mean anything! Although this hybrid sounds similar to what Chrysler has proposed for the Dodge Durango, no hardware existed when this patent application was made. In my short search; I found two other patents which describe a hybrid vehicle which drives one axle with an engine and the other with an electric motor. Both of these were issued long before Mr. *Smore*'s. The reality is; this is the first idea someone comes up with when thinking up a hybrid vehicle. This is exactly what I describe when I describe basically what a hybrid vehicle is in a coming chapter. Chrysler would never prevail in court with this one. But Mr. *Smore* got a handsome bonus. This one is a gem!

Well it's easy to get a patent! *Dee Lusion* knew this! To *Dee*, the definition of a man seems to be "who has the most patents?" I don't know how many he held, but it appeared the number was approaching triple digits. I can't recall if any of his patents were actually used on products in the market. It seems that similar to the patent for the rubber suspension, most of them were for devices which either didn't work or didn't work as well as current systems available. It seems he searched out the most asinine way to do something, insuring no one else had done it, and patented it. It is easy to get a patent for something stupid. Everyone else thinks it's stupid, and they don't bother to file for a patent (I'm falsely assuming that it hasn't been patented before). I'm surprised he doesn't hold a patent for a square wheel.

TRIZ training

TRIZ is an acronym from some Russian words which describes a method for inventing things. You didn't know you could take a class and learn to become an inventor did you? Well the leaders of technological advancement over there in Russia had just the system. Then Chrysler hired these goons to teach it to us. What these gentlemen had done; was analyze many inventions and had come up with a theory on how to invent other things based on the research. They had not invented anything themselves mind you, except for this theory which they thrusted upon us.

Some useful information was gleaned from this weeklong class. The thing I remember most was; 95 percent of patents are of little benefit to society. They are usually just a way to accomplish a task differently that is already accomplished adequately, or something that doesn't even work. The other 5 percent of patents are better ways of accomplishing tasks which are already accomplished. These are the patents that can make corporations or individuals wealthy. A very small percentage of patents will create a whole new industry, i.e., the computer, airplanes, etc. The bottom line is it's easy to get a patent, especially if you've done a stupid design. So having a bunch of patents just means you spend a lot of time with a patent attorney. Mr. *Lusion* provided substantial evidence for this theory.

Many useful patents suffer from the "not invented here" syndrome, and never benefit anyone until much later when the inventor becomes more important, or he dies and no longer can be flattered. One such example is photo copying. The process was originally invented at Kodak. Kodak would not pursue it. Xerox later made an industry out of this technology.

Patent awards and important people

Chrysler offered incentives for employees to patent their ideas, and would hold a banquet each year to honor those who had had patents issued. Chrysler owned the patents as the inventions were created while you were in their employ. A high ranking executive would always be the keynote speaker; I think Lee Iacocca even spoke at one once. I went to one where the keynote speaker was Bob Lutz, then the No. 2 man at Chrysler. At each table were seated several employees and guests and one Chrysler executive. I suppose the idea was to let us rub shoulders with upper management.

The executive seated at my table was the Human Resources VP, a woman. After my dining experience, I concluded she was a product of Chrysler's affirmative action program. She was the only woman at any of the big three which held a vice president position. Her husband was a lesser executive at GM. The conversation at the table that night did not give me the impression she really had the authority her position should command. She was a socialite put in this position as a corporate ornament.

I grew up in what you might call a slightly upper middle-class home. I have dreamed of wealth and fame, like being a championship race car driver, and when I was a naive young engineer I'd dreamed of running a car company myself. Living in Detroit, I had the opportunity to associate with and observe some "very powerful" people. The female executive and Mr. Lutz at the patent awards banquet are two examples. When I was leaving that night, I had to wait a few minutes for the elevator. Mrs. Lutz was also waiting. While I was admiring the fine work of some plastic surgeon, our eyes met briefly. I think I saw the saddest person I've ever seen in my life. Sometimes in my life I wished I was another person, but it was always someone that had a less complicated life than mine. Of all the socialites which I had met since moving to Detroit, never did I wish I was any one of them. It was usually pity I felt for their unhappy lives, such as I felt for Mrs. Lutz that night while waiting for the elevator.

One holiday season at Liberty, I got a curious invitation on the corporate email to a "Christmas" gathering at the home of a Chrysler VP. I had grown up in Utah and of course I was a Mormon. This vice president was also a Mormon, and only those employees at Chrysler who were Mormons were invited to the gathering. This seemed to smack a little bit of religious discrimination in the workplace. Nonetheless, it was a good opportunity for a date as I was still single. Additionally it was an opportunity to see my old roommate, the "light bulb changing" challenged one. So I went. The VP's home seemed very artificial and vacant. I didn't want to be him either.

Another very powerful Mormon was George Romney and likewise I felt pity for him and his family. Powerful people never seem to be very happy. I had a conversation once with an old marine mechanic who lived on the Clinton River near Detroit. He said, "The bigger the boat, the bigger the frown." He would see some grumpy old dude in his 60 foot yacht growling at all the other boats, but four kids in a rubber dinghy laughing their heads off. My boat is 8 feet 4 inches!

A new suspension concept

Often outside inventors would invent something they would like to sell to Chrysler. The really promising technology such as the kinetic suspension which I have previously mentioned is taken directly to the design groups. When the design groups aren't interested, but someone of some influence such as Francios Castaing is interested or owes a fellow countryman a favor; the task of developing the technology is given to Liberty. Little did these inventors know, when development is given to Liberty, it had no hope in becoming integrated into Chrysler's products. The Design departments always applied the "not invented here" principle to anything done at Liberty. So not just people were "shoved aside," and sent to Liberty, ideas were too. One such invention was the "Contractive Suspension." The inventor was a Frenchman who was a former Formula One race car driver.

To understand the contractive suspension and its benefits, one must understand how an anti-sway bar works on an automobile. Essentially when the car is doing a cornering maneuver, weight is transferred from the inside tires to the outside tires. The suspension on the side of the vehicle with the additional weight will move into "jounce" travel. The side where weight is removed goes into "rebound" travel. The resulting effect on the vehicle is called "body roll." To reduce the amount of body roll, the anti-sway bar dramatically increases the spring rate at each wheel in the roll condition; keeping the vehicle more nearly flat.

The contractive suspension had the same effect as it dramatically increased the spring rate at the wheel where weight was removed, thus the wheel moves dramatically less into "rebound" travel and the spring rate is unchanged at the wheel which receives the weight. This also had the effect of keeping the vehicle nearly flat. In addition, it lowered the vehicle's center of gravity in a cornering maneuver. Consequently enhancing the vehicle's cornering capability. The inventors also claimed it would be a cost savings because the anti-sway bars were no longer necessary.

The engineer I replaced at Liberty had the inventor install the system on a Chrysler Intrepid over in France. He made a trip over to France, and gave glowing reports of how wonderful the suspension system was. I think it was the French wine. The parts were removed from the vehicle in France, and were shipped to me. I had them installed on a Dodge Intrepid in our fleet. I was not so impressed. The vehicle made a lot of clunking noises. I did find conditions where I could convince myself handling was improved.

In the meantime, the inventors had come up with an improved design of this system, so we decided to give it another shot. We had it installed on a vehicle, again an Intrepid. Instead of just shipping the parts back, we had the entire vehicle shipped back after they completed development in France. Before the vehicle was to be shipped back, I first took a trip to France to drive the vehicle there.

Pilot

Ever since my first mini bike, I would define myself as a motorized recreationalist. I loved driving fast. In the United States, opportunities for motorized recreation are not on our highways. Fifteen speeding tickets in my life cured me of this, now I drive a 4wd SUV. Now I speed only on the snow or on the water. However, if I lived in France, I would get a sports car. It appeared to me that you could drive them as intended often enough to make it worthwhile.

For the week I was there, I drove an Intrepid to the limit of its capabilities. The test fleet included the modified Intrepid, an unmodified Intrepid, and a simple French sedan with the contractive suspension added. The four drivers were the inventor (a retired F1 driver), his assistant, a European automotive journalist (also a former F1 "pilot") and me. On their freeway I had the Intrepid at over 140 mph, about all it could do. But the real fun was on the mountain roads in the south of France; passing slower cars when you can only see 100 yards before the next turn in the road or passing a big Mercedes coming the other way at 30 mph with only inches to spare on a narrow twisty mountain road. The biggest shot to my ego was when the old F1 pilot asked me, "Who did you pilot for?" In Europe, a race car driver is called a "Pilot." F1 is the pinnacle of the sport.

Once we had the Intrepid back in the states, several demonstrations were arranged. I couldn't get any interest from anyone in the design groups. They all indicated they had too much work on their plates already and had no time to consider using this new technology. I didn't have the authority or the sales skills to get anyone interested. Eventually the new suspension was no longer pursued. In analyzing this invention from the perspective of my TRIZ training, I believe it is an improvement over the current practice in the industry. However the improvement was not significant enough to overcome the "not invented here" syndrome. I suppose the technology may someday be adopted by someone in the industry, but probably not before the death of the inventor. Just like artists, death likely will accelerate an inventor's notoriety.

Part 5

HYBRID ELECTRIC VEHICLES

Chapter 19

CHRYSLER'S HYBRIDS

Al Gore's vision

As I have previously mentioned, Steve Spencer was brought on board to head up the Chrysler HEV program. Just a little background: several years earlier, pressure was put on the U.S. automakers particularly in California to develop zero emissions vehicles, or in other words electric cars. But by the mid-1990s, it was clear the public would not embrace this technology. Essentially electric cars are like regular cars with tiny little gas tanks that take several hours to refill. It takes about 1000 pounds of batteries to store the same amount of energy contained in one gallon of gasoline (which weighs about seven pounds). Back to my earlier discussion on reliability; this makes an electric vehicle only about 10 percent as reliable as a gasoline powered car, the "planned interruption" to recharge the batteries is very severe. The reality that electric vehicles were not the future was finally accepted by those who promoted the development of zero emissions vehicles, including one of the chief of these, Al Gore, the Vice President at the time.

In Al Gore's book, <u>Earth In The Balance,</u> he states in reference to the automobile; "We now know that their cumulative impact on the global environment is posing a mortal threat to the security of every nation that is more deadly than that of any military enemy we are ever again likely to confront." He called for the elimination of the internal combustion engine in 25 years (10 years ago). It was Mr. Gore's vision to pool the best resources of the U.S. government and the U.S. automakers to develop a supercar capable of getting up to 80 miles per gallon as a first step in the elimination of internal combustion engines. And this wouldn't be no sissy car either; it would have the same roominess and performance of the Ford Taurus.

Similar to how the last notable Democratic administration had pooled the nation's resources to put a man on the moon; the great accomplishment of this administration would be the development of a "Supercar." Since the Cold War was over, the national labs which had in the past concentrated their research for defense purposes could now pool their resources to peacetime activities and aid the U.S. automakers in this development. The big three U.S. automakers would partner with the National Research Laboratories of the government and cooperatively share all this new technology thus leaping ahead of their European and Japanese counterparts. This group was formally organized as the Partnership for a New Generation of Vehicles (PNGV). Now to me, this sounded quite appealing. This fit right in with my dreams; to be instrumental in revolutionizing the way Americans drive.

Flawed vision

However, there were some flaws with this vision. The first is the auto industry is extremely competitive. U.S. automakers never share anything unless it is stolen or they are paid a lot for it. A second flaw is, referring back to Eskelson's principle #2; the best and brightest scientists are not government employees at the national labs. A third flaw; with gas prices so cheap in North America, there really is not a market for high mileage vehicles. An argument can be made that Europe and Japan may have such a market. So this vision of Mr. Gore's was really more like a fantasy. Recently in my local paper, the editor wrote an opinion piece about hybrids and summarized, "This may be a dream. But what a dream!"

The supercar program was to be administered through the Department of Energy (DOE). Each automaker would enter into a contract with the DOE to develop hybrid vehicle technology. The program was to be a 50/50 cost sharing program. This means taxpayers pay half and the automakers would pay the other half. It looked a little bit (a lot) like corporate welfare. Thus, Chrysler was reluctant to participate. They were the last to sign a contract with the DOE. Before the contract was signed, we had many discussions among those in our department about the ethics of working on such a program. We thought it was a rip off of the American taxpayers. Nobody strongly agreed that hybrids were viable. There even were some who indicated they would take a high moral road and get transferred to a different department at Chrysler.

Both General Motors and Ford signed contracts that were well into the triple digits of millions of dollars. Chrysler's initial proposal was only a double-digit number of millions, which truly would have made the General Motors and Ford contracts look like corporate welfare. So pressure was brought against Chrysler to increase the value of their contract. The final contract which Chrysler signed was over $100 million. To Chrysler's credit, they did try to show restraint when it came to spending the American taxpayer dollars. The National Renewable Energy Lab (NREL) in Golden, Colorado was a part of the DOE and would administer the contract.

None of the big three automakers were looking for corporate welfare at the time, record profits at all three were occurring. The reason for these profits was because gas was cheap and Americans were buying bigger cars, namely sport utility vehicles and trucks. The Clinton-Gore administration was proposing stricter emission standards and an increase in CAFE (corporate average fuel economy) standards. The big three automakers by participating in the DOE HEV programs were able to get the administration to remove pressure for the increased CAFE standard. For this reason I, and others who thought the program was immoral, could find a justification to participate in it. No one left the team after the contract was signed as some had threatened.

The Chrysler HEV team

The Chrysler HEV contract was not Chrysler's first foray into hybrid vehicle technology. However the previous attempts seem to have been an embarrassment to Chrysler's upper management. Hence Steve Spencer was brought in to head up the program. His right hand man was Steve Harding. Harding had worked previously on Chrysler's electric vehicle programs and was an electrical engineer. In addition to his electrical engineering skills, he was an excellent administrator. He was immensely valuable to Mr. Spencer.

Bob *"Leery"* was an enthusiastic new graduate of Chrysler's engineering training program, and had not yet established an engineering specialty. His education was in mechanical engineering.

There were others on the team. I only mention one other because he was the "Ph.D. idiot" I got one piece of good advice from. Otherwise he was influential in my expansion of Eskelson's "Principle #2" (those with unnecessary degrees are idiots). I initially did not do much work on the HEV contract as my time was used on the CCV program and other chassis projects.

Chrysler's HEV experience

Previous to the signing of the HEV contract, the team at Liberty had been working on a few hybrid projects. One had begun and since been abandoned before I arrived at Liberty. However, due to the "Liberty" method, there was still ample evidence the stories I heard were true. Since these were drivetrain projects, they were directed by *Dim Wiser*.

One was nicknamed the "Rubber Band Car." Remember when you were kids, and you got the little balsa wood airplane with the propeller. How was that propeller powered? By a rubber band (in the instructions for the toy airplane, it is called a "motor band"). The idea of a hybrid electric vehicle is that you take some of the kinetic energy (energy because of the vehicle's momentum) and recover it and store it to be reused later. The only known effective method for doing this is to store the energy in batteries. As I mentioned with electric vehicles, batteries are very heavy and can not hold very much energy, so an alternative to batteries to store energy was a "Holy Grail" of hybrid research.

Dim was thinking outside the box, perhaps rubber bands would be a better device to store energy. He was probably thinking; "Heck, if it can store energy to "motor" a toy airplane, why can't it store energy to "motor" a car? The energy to power a car is much greater, so we just need some great big rubber bands. This is so brilliant; I'm surprised no one has thought of this before!" It seems many of the "brilliant" ideas at Liberty were inspired by toys. The process of molding the body on the CCV was inspired by a toy car!

Dim Smore and *Dim Wiser* were so impressed with their brilliance; they are so much smarter than everyone else on the planet. They must have thought, "This was a breakthrough and would revolutionize the automotive world! We need to build a car right away to demonstrate this breakthrough technology." So the new drivetrain was quickly designed and fitted to a vehicle. I don't remember the exact number, but 5 or 6 long tubes which would contain the huge rubber bands extended the length of the car. Then these would be connected to a transmission which would wind up the rubber bands when you stopped. When you wanted to go, the rubber bands were unleashed to assist the engine in powering the car.

One thing with toys, they usually get broken (mine always did!). The rubber bands on these little balsa wood airplanes broke after a few flights. Sometimes they broke when you were winding up the propeller and it hurt. Now imagine a big rubber band about six feet long, one inch thick and four inches wide and how it might hurt when it breaks. "Oh we can develop a new rubber that will be durable." must've been the thoughts of those more brilliant than me. Well, rubber bands were never installed into the car.

However, the employees at Liberty had to endure several months of large explosions in the rubber band test fixture in the lab at the back of the building. This was part of the "Liberty Way"; congratulate yourself for your own brilliance and quickly build the hardware to demonstrate the newly thought up technology before any of it is proven.

In any other research organization, perhaps rubber experts would be consulted to determine feasibility of durable rubber bands. Then they would be designed, developed and proven before additional expenditures occurred. But then other research organizations didn't have the "brilliant" men leading them that Liberty had. The rubber band car became what is known as a pushcar (I personally pushed it once). Whenever it needed to be moved, it had to be pushed. The car should've been crushed; but *Dim* and *Dim* still were hoping for a breakthrough of durable rubber bands and kept the car around just in case. Even though *Dim Wiser* never laughed, this program brought a lot of laughter to the rest of the Liberty staff after they had run for cover following an explosion.

The Patriot racecar

The Chrysler hybrid research project when I arrived at Liberty was the Chrysler Patriot racecar. *Dim Wiser* must have been playing with a top when he came up with this one. It would showcase the "ultimate" in hybrid technology. Like the rubber band car, this also was never more than a pushcar. The car never moved under its own power despite the videos which you might have seen showing it driving around a racetrack. A tow strap and some clever editing were used to create these videos. Unlike the rubber band car, this one was shown to the public to garner some PR. This was the current project being led by *Dim* when I came to Liberty.

I will attempt to give a clear description of hybrid technology in coming pages as there are many different types of hybrid vehicles. The Patriot racecar was essentially what is called a "series hybrid." There were three major components which made up the drivetrain; the traction motor (electric motor to drive the tires), a flywheel to store the energy (instead of batteries), and the generator driven by some type of turbine engine (to provide energy for storage in the flywheel). None of these components were ever developed enough to ever be installed in an operational car. Thus the Patriot ever remained a pushcar, even when a second one was built.

The flywheel was hyped as an alternative to batteries as an energy storage device. The flywheel for the Patriot racecar needed to store enough energy to power a 500 plus horsepower electric motor. I won't try to explain the design details of a flywheel at this time. I will however, try to illustrate the energy it would be required to contain. Imagine a fully loaded semi truck traveling at 100 miles an hour down a steep mountain freeway in Colorado. If it is skillfully steered, it will arrive at the bottom of the mountain safely. But not every trip will be successful, an error will be made and a fiery crash will occur. A flywheel is a kinetic energy storage device; a fully loaded semi truck traveling at 100 miles an hour also contains a tremendous amount (about the same amount as the Patriot's flywheel) of kinetic energy. Thus any errors have disastrous results.

The testing of flywheels destroyed the interior of several test cells. One technician gave his life when a flywheel in a test cell disintegrated. This event dampened the enthusiasm for flywheels.

On a dynamometer, the Patriot electric motor was operated at about 50 percent power. I don't recall any information regarding the turbine. But as if Chrysler hadn't spent enough money on this foolishness, a second Patriot racecar was built. It was a neat looking pushcar too.

Joining the Chrysler HEV team

I suppose these two examples of *Dim Wiser's* brilliance did not qualify him to head up the contract with the DOE. With my criticism of the rubber suspension on the CCV and my subsequent loss of responsibility for that system, I was searching to find some new responsibilities that would not require me to be working with *Dee* or *Dim*. Perhaps there was something I could do on the HEV program. There was very little chassis work required.

Under the DOE contract, part of the development process involved doing computer simulation of an HEV. Unlike the Liberty way, it was hoped through computer simulation, a workable hybrid could be optimized before any hardware was built and tested. Chrysler had a group called "Scientific Laboratories" which had people that specialized in doing computer modeling of vehicle systems. They had computer models that simulated engine performance, fuel economy, engine emissions, vehicle dynamic performance, etc. But they did not have a lot of people with this expertise, and we could not get the support from this group which we desired. An employee at NREL also developed a simple computer model to simulate an HEV. However he had little knowledge in the design and operation of automobiles. Bob *Leery* had been our liaison in getting the simulation done at NREL and with our scientific laboratories group.

I observed Bob's frustration in this and came up with a solution. I volunteered to learn to do simulation and take on this responsibility. You may recall I had envisioned a time when all design and development of new cars would take place in the virtual world. Here was an opportunity for me to further my vision, though it was not in my specialty of chassis systems.

It was determined our HEV computer model would be developed in the MatLab/SimuLink software currently available for PCs. This was the same software used for the NREL model. Both Bob and I received training in the software and we started to develop our own internal simulation program or model.

Not long after we began, most of the simulation work was done by me. Several months later, the team totally relied on me for simulation work. Since simulation required a thorough understanding of all the vehicle systems involved, I became very knowledgeable of hybrid vehicles. When I left Chrysler, I probably knew more about hybrid vehicles than anyone

114

else in the Corporation and probably with the exception of a few, anyone else in the world. This is why I can intelligently write about hybrids. I suppose you could call me an expert.

Chapter 20

WHAT IS A HYBRID?

Energy Conversion

Are you sleepy yet, take some Nodoz for this section or you will be. To understand what a hybrid is, I need to first teach about "energy" and "energy conversion." If you understand this, hybrids are easy to comprehend. If the physics here are too much, skip to the last four sections of the chapter and read the summaries about hybrids.

Energy exists in many forms. I've touched on "kinetic" energy, which is the energy of a mass in motion like my 100 mph semi-truck. It is more commonly known as momentum. "Electricity" and "work" are also forms of energy. "Heat" is another form of energy. Work is a force over a certain distance. Work is done to get a vehicle in motion, resulting in it possessing "kinetic" energy.

Another energy form required for this discussion is what is called "potential" energy. Electricity and work cannot be stored. Potential energy can be stored. This comes in the form of gasoline or chemicals in batteries as it relates to vehicles. Potential energy is also contained in firewood, coal or anything else we call fuel. Potential energy is very useful in that it can be stored.

It is possible to store heat and kinetic energy, but usually not for a long period of time. And it can be dangerous. Both the rubber band and flywheel are kinetic energy storage devices. In small amounts, such as the toy airplane, storing energy this way is relatively safe. However, storing large amounts of kinetic energy leads to disaster as demonstrated by Mr. *Wiser*. The safest way to store energy is with potential energy, though it has potential pitfalls too. Ever see a house burn down? This is the potential energy in the wood being converted to heat.

"Machines" are energy conversion devices. Usually a machine is required to convert one form of energy to another form of energy. An exception is in the creation of heat, such as lighting a match to gasoline. This will cause an energy conversion of the gasoline to heat (no machine here). However for all energy conversions to take place, energy must be expended.

A very simple machine, such as a lever, takes energy in the form of work, such as a man pushing with a force over a certain distance, and converts this work to a much more powerful force over a smaller distance. This machine did not change the energy to a different form; it converted work to work. In a car, a similar energy conversion (work to work) takes place in the transmission. The lever and transmission are "energy conversion devices."

For "potential" energy to do work, a more sophisticated energy conversion device is usually required. The internal combustion engine converts the potential energy of gasoline to work. A battery converts the potential energy in it's chemicals to electricity.

An automobile is a conglomeration of energy conversion devices. The battery converts its potential energy to electricity. The starter motor converts this electricity to work and cranks the engine. The engine then converts the potential energy in gasoline to work. The transmission converts work to work. Axles convert work to work. Tires convert work to kinetic energy. Automobile brakes convert kinetic energy to heat (actually tires convert the kinetic energy back to work, and then the brakes convert the work to heat). There are many kinds of "energy conversions" in a car; these are only a few examples.

One (the only one!) advantage of a hybrid vehicle is it can recover some of the kinetic energy and store it to be used later. With the exception of rubber bands and flywheels, this is done by converting the work to electricity and storing it in batteries. There are other methods being tried as you read, but an understanding of these isn't necessary here.

A basic car, in terms of significant energy conversion devices, is: the gas tank (energy storage device), the engine (energy conversion device), and the transmission (energy conversion device). In comparison, an electric car is: the batteries (energy storage and conversion device), and the electric motor (energy conversion device). Less significant are tires, driveshafts, etc. Since these components are common to all vehicles, they are omitted in further discussion.

Efficiency

Whenever a machine converts energy, some of the energy put into the machine will be converted to heat. The remaining energy is converted to the form of energy resulting from the machine. The formula "energy in = energy out + heat" describes all energy conversions. The energy out is always less than the energy in because there is always some heat created. Efficiency is the formula "energy out ÷ energy in" and is always less than 100 percent.

In the case of a lever, a minute amount of heat from friction will be created at the fulcrum and a greater force with less distance results (the form of energy in work). Efficiency will be nearly 100 percent because the heat created is imperceptible. The form of energy "work," in this example is a force over a distance. In the case of an engine, work is defined by torque and speed.

An internal combustion engine creates a lot of heat. So efficiency is much less than 100 percent. At full power, efficiency is about 30 percent. At less than full power, efficiency can be less than 20 percent. The average efficiency in a typical car is a little better than 20 percent. Then the energy conversion through a transmission is somewhat less than 100 percent. So on average, less than 20 percent of the potential energy stored in the gasoline is converted to work to move the car.

Work can also undergo an energy conversion and be stored. The work from an engine can power an alternator which converts it to electricity which then converts the chemicals in a battery and energy is stored. Every time an energy conversion takes place, some energy is converted to heat and is lost. The lever with nearly 100 percent efficiency creates very little heat. The engine with only 20 percent efficiency creates a lot of heat. Energy conversion efficiencies in vehicles are typically between 20 and nearly 100 percent.

Let's examine the energy conversion process for an electric car. The potential energy is stored in the batteries, an energy conversion takes place, and electricity is created. The electric motor converts the electricity to work and the vehicle is propelled. In fact the electric vehicle has some advantages. The average total efficiency of these energy conversions can be better than 70 percent. And, some of the kinetic energy of the moving vehicle can be converted back to electricity and converted to potential energy and stored in the batteries though regenerative braking. The only disadvantage of an electric vehicle is relative to gasoline, only a very small amount of energy can be stored on the vehicle. Then the time to refill this stored energy is significant. It takes about 1000 pounds of batteries to store as much energy as one gallon of gasoline. It is impressive an electric vehicle can travel nearly 100 miles on this amount of energy. A similar gas powered car with average efficiency of 20 percent, would only travel 25 miles on this same amount of energy.

Regenerative Braking

As I refer to regenerative braking many times, let's review exactly what it is. It is the process where a vehicle's kinetic energy is converted and stored for use later. The tires are hooked to a generator which does an energy conversion to electricity while slowing the car down; which is then stored in the batteries with a second energy conversion.

If you have ever ridden a bicycle with a generator operated light, you noticed when you turned it on, it slowed the bicycle down or it became harder to pedal. This is regenerative braking. Except instead of converting the electricity to potential energy and storing it, it uses the electricity to operate the bicycle's light. To stop a vehicle without regenerative braking, the vehicle brake system converts the vehicle's kinetic energy to heat. Then the energy is lost forever.

Batteries

Batteries are amazing devices. They are not only an "energy storage" device, but also an "energy conversion" device. The problem with batteries is they do not have the capacity to store huge amounts of energy. If a battery could be invented that could store "huge" amounts, it would make someone very wealthy. All three automakers and academics around the world were searching for such a battery breakthrough. This would dramatically improve the range for electric vehicles. No breakthroughs have occurred; though on occasion I heard rumors that something may be imminent.

One indication the big three automakers were not serious about hybrid electric vehicles was the fact they entered into cooperative programs with the U.S. government. If the automakers had thought there was a future with hybrid vehicles (meaning they could make money by producing them), they certainly wouldn't want to share the technology with each other and the government. When any of the three automakers had promising technology, they went to great lengths to keep it secret from the other two automakers. That would include keeping it secret from the government (the government would just give it to everyone). A breakthrough would mean huge profits for the company with that technology.

An example of this was some battery technology for which Chrysler had purchased patent rights. They kept this a secret from the other automakers and the government. Its development looked promising and would be the breakthrough that would make electric vehicles viable. It was shared with us at Liberty because the team working on the technology had become optimistic a breakthrough was imminent. Since Chrysler has canceled electric vehicle programs, I assume the imminent breakthrough has not occurred.

Hybrids

A conventional gasoline powered automobile is terribly inefficient compared to an electric vehicle. Its only advantage is it can carry a tremendous amount of potential energy (the gas tank). It usually can travel more than 300 miles before needing to be refilled. An electric car can only hold the energy of about 1 gallon of gasoline in its batteries. It is very efficient and goes almost 100 miles on this amount of energy. Refilling (charging the batteries) the electric car takes hours (not just minutes like the gasoline powered car). Note a battery breakthrough would make the electric car be as convenient as a gas car. Then the idea of a hybrid would not be considered.

A hybrid vehicle is the combination of an electric and conventional car. It has a gas tank and gasoline engine, and batteries with an electric motor. In terms of energy conversion devices: it has two "energy storage devices" (gas tank and batteries) and "four energy conversion devices" (engine, transmission, batteries and electric motor). This is the simplest form of a hybrid. Referring back to *Dim Smore's* "Environmentally Sensitive Hybrid," it could be a vehicle with an engine and transmission to drive the front wheels and with an electric motor to drive the rear wheels. With a gasoline tank, the vehicle can travel very far without having to recharge the batteries. With the energy in the batteries, the car can be driven with the electric motor and not put out any emissions.

The problem is, with two of everything, it weighs more than either car. Fuel economy suffers with the extra weight and consequently it pollutes more when driven on gas. When driven on electric, the batteries don't last as long because of the extra work to propel an additional engine, transmission and gas tank. Even with regenerative braking, the electric range is still compromised compared to an electric vehicle. So it pollutes more than a regular car and won't go as far. We didn't improve on either characteristic. As stupid as this is, there were academics at some universities (and some in the industry) writing papers (patents) about the virtues of such a vehicle.

The series hybrid

The object of a hybrid electric vehicle is to combine the advantages of an electric vehicle and the advantages of a conventional vehicle, not the disadvantages of both. The advantages of an electric vehicle are improved efficiency enhanced by regenerative braking and zero emissions. The advantages of a conventional vehicle are the long-range and the ability to quickly refuel.

An electric vehicle "kook" at the time had converted a small Honda car to an electric and was driving it across the country to demonstrate the viability of electric cars. However, in order to not "run out of gas", he towed a trailer which contained a gasoline engine which powered a generator which kept his batteries charged. It no longer was a zero emissions vehicle. It became a hybrid when the trailer was added. It had two energy storage devices; the gas tank and batteries. And four energy conversion devices; an engine, batteries, generator and drive motor. Note this hybrid configuration replaces the transmission from the previous configuration with a generator.

Stuffing the contents of the trailer in the trunk of the electric car is the "series" hybrid configuration.

All the technology presently exists; "Why haven't we seen any series hybrids on the road?" you might ask. Common sense would deduce, "economy doesn't improve when you are towing a trailer."

However, there is an advantage to this type of hybrid. With the ability to store energy in the batteries, the engine can be operated at full power where efficiency is 30 percent. The extra power not required to drive the car is then stored in the batteries. When the batteries are fully charged, the engine is shut off and the vehicle is driven electrically. When the charge in the batteries gets low, the engine is started and run at full power to recharge them. In a vehicle like this, the engine is always operated at 30 percent efficiency which is a 50 percent improvement over the average efficiency of a conventional vehicle at 20 percent.

Again many papers were written by "experts" at our universities espousing these facts and the virtues of the series hybrid. However, let's look at the efficiency of the entire series hybrid vehicle compared to a gasoline powered car.

Series hybrid efficiency

As I have previously explained, an automobile is a conglomeration of "energy conversion" devices. Every time energy is converted, heat is created and some energy is lost. A traditional gasoline powered automobile is on average about 20 percent efficient. This is done with two significant energy conversions (in the engine and transmission). The insignificant energy conversions are like a lever with nearly 100 percent efficiency and therefore are not included in this discussion.

Let's thoroughly examine the case of the series hybrid: It has four significant energy conversion devices. The gasoline engine, a generator, batteries and drive motor.

The gasoline engine operated at peak efficiency won't meet emission standards. And engines only operate at this efficiency when they have been fully warmed up. So when the batteries get low and the engine is restarted, it will not run at peak efficiency until it reaches its proper operating temperature. So engine efficiency under actual operating conditions in a series hybrid vehicle which meets emission standards will be more in the range of 25 to 28 percent. It's still better than 20 percent.

I'll be optimistic and say the series hybrid engine will <u>convert</u> gasoline to work at an average efficiency of 28 percent while operating the generator. The generator then <u>converts</u> the work to electricity at probably about 95 percent efficiency. For comparison purposes, we will assume the power requirements are those of the EPA city/highway test cycles combined. Because the car only rarely requires high power, it does not require all of the electricity being generated to power the car. So the excess electricity is <u>converted</u> again and stored in the battery at probably 95 percent efficiency. When the batteries are fully charged, then the generator will shut down. Then the energy to power the car will be drawn out of the batteries with a chemical to electricity <u>conversion</u> at about 95 percent efficiency. Then the traction motor will <u>convert</u> the energy to power the car. The regenerative breaking can improve the vehicle efficiency by maybe five percent. So figuring this into the traction motor efficiency, we will be generous and say its efficiency is 80 percent on average.

Now I know this is a lot of numbers to digest. Not counting regenerative braking (this is added to the efficiency of the electric motor), five "energy conversions" have taken place before the car is powered. Combining the efficiencies of the five energy conversions (.28 X .95 X .95 X .95 X .80) results in overall efficiency of only 19 percent for the series hybrid. This is worse than the conventional car at 20 percent. And I'm being optimistic. Additionally, the hybrid has an extra motor and batteries (it is heavier); more work must be done to operate it. So in the case of the series hybrid using a gasoline engine, it uses more gas than a conventional vehicle and thus produces more emissions also. The standard gasoline car wins the efficiency game because it has only two energy conversions compared to the five for a series hybrid.

This example is using the EPA combined city/highway tests for fuel economy. Strictly on the city test, the series hybrid would do just slightly better than a conventional car, primarily because much energy is recovered through brake regeneration. Strictly on the highway test, the series hybrid does much worse.

More efficient engines

Now the gasoline engine is not the most efficient energy conversion device available. The diesel engine can convert the potential energy from diesel fuel at a peak efficiency of over 40 percent. But diesel engines have inherent drawbacks that have prevented widespread acceptance in the marketplace.

We often called them "stinky, dirty diesels." Meeting emission standards with a diesel is more difficult than with the gas engine. Diesel engines also are slower to produce power than gas. They can make as much power, but take more time to go from low to high power. Improvements in this area have been made, yet the advantage remains with gas engines. This characteristic has slowed acceptance in regular vehicles, but would not be a handicap in a series hybrid. A series hybrid with a diesel engine powering the generator would be more efficient than a gas powered car. But then a conventional diesel powered car is still more efficient than the diesel powered hybrid. So a diesel powered series hybrid doesn't make sense either.

Gas turbine technology at the time and for the previous 30 years could do an energy conversion of gasoline to work at slightly over 30 percent efficiency at peak power. In theory, if ceramic components could be developed to replace some of the metal components in a gas turbine, efficiency for gas turbines could be in excess of 40 percent. Just like the battery technology, a technological breakthrough was imminent for the past 30 years. In the General Motors contract, there was a huge budget to pursue this technological breakthrough. This didn't make a lot of sense to me and others, particularly since strategies to control emissions on diesels had been developed. A breakthrough in gas turbine technology would make it as good as existing diesel technology. Eventually the General Motors turbine program was dropped. Nevertheless a lot of people had got their paychecks from working on the program.

Series hybrids don't make sense. This is why there is not one available on the market today.

Chapter 21

A BETTER HYBRID

Parallel hybrids

There are other types of hybrids. In the discussion of the series hybrid, I have illustrated there is not a benefit to doing such a hybrid. This is because there are too many "energy conversions." With each conversion, efficiency is reduced. Some of the energy is recovered through regenerative braking, but not enough to make up for the disadvantage of the multiple energy conversions.

Another type of hybrid is called the "parallel" hybrid. This is the type the "Environmentally Sensitive Hybrid" would be classified as. It consists of a conventional drivetrain in parallel to an electric vehicle drivetrain. The vehicle can be driven by the conventional drivetrain or the electric drivetrain or both. I previously dismissed this configuration because of the significant weight added with the extra components. However, if the components are resized, a benefit to such a hybrid may be realized under certain driving conditions. If you are driving down a freeway at 65 mph, the hybrid will always have worse fuel economy than a comparable non-hybrid vehicle because of the weight disadvantage.

If the engine is made smaller, then it will be operated nearer its peak power under lighter loads than in a conventional car. With only two energy conversions, efficiency is improved. However, with the extra weight of batteries and electric motor, overall fuel economy will not improve. Because the vehicle is "underpowered," on occasions when additional power is required, the electric drivetrain will assist. Additionally, efficiency of the engine conversion of gasoline can be enhanced by increasing the load on the gas engine. This is done by powering a generator and storing the electricity created in the batteries. This energy will undergo five conversions before powering the car, but the energy is only a small portion of the energy used.

The disadvantage of this design is the increased weight. With smaller components, the increased weight is minimal. The combined power of both the gas and electric drivetrain provides for the equivalent power of a standard car. The car would be lighter than a full hybrid, but still be heavier than a standard car. In stop and go driving conditions, the ability for regenerative braking makes it possible to improve overall fuel economy.

Kinetic energy converted through brake regeneration is stored in the batteries. This is the big payoff for such a hybrid. In a conventional vehicle, the energy is just turned to heat by the brakes and lost forever. Even though four energy conversions are required to use regenerated energy to power the car, it is still better than not having it. So the advantage of a parallel hybrid is; kinetic energy normally lost on a conventional vehicle is recovered and used later to power the car. This is a very generic description. In summary; the parallel hybrid typically uses only 2 energy conversions to power itself (having the advantage of minimal energy conversions like a conventional car), and with the ability to recapture kinetic energy through brake regeneration to use again. With the additional weight, this is only an advantage when kinetic energy is recovered (such as in city stop and go driving).

Civic hybrid

There are three hybrids on the market today, all Japanese (so much for the PNGV leaping the US automakers ahead); the Toyota Prius, Honda Civic and Honda Insight. All are parallel hybrids. For comparison's sake, let's examine the Civic and the Civic hybrid to see the advantage of the parallel system.

First we'll review the operation of the conventional vehicle. The basic Civic is about 2500 lbs., with a 115 horsepower engine. Only occasionally will the driver require the full 115 horsepower. The average horsepower requirement is probably more like 15 horsepower, 13 percent of the engine's peak horsepower. The engine must be sized at 115 horsepower for the occasions when 115 horsepower is required. So the average efficiency of the engine in doing the energy conversion to work from gasoline will be the efficiency at 15 horsepower which is about 20 percent.

The parallel hybrid vehicle will be the same size and have the same performance as our 2500 lb. car with a 115 horsepower engine. In this car we use an 85 horsepower gasoline engine and a 15 horsepower electric motor for a total of 100 horsepower. With the additional batteries, this vehicle weighs 200 lbs more at 2700 lbs. This may raise a question, "this vehicle is heavier with less total horsepower; performance will not be equivalent?"

Here is an advantage of electric motors, they can produce tremendous amounts of torque at low speed, and therefore torque available to accelerate the vehicle will be as good as with the 115 hp engine. Top speed will be compromised, but it is assumed you don't have a need for top speed. With the electric motor torque available at low speed, this lowers the low speed torque requirement for the gasoline engine. The engine can be further optimized for efficiency at lighter loads.

Now the average horsepower requirement for this parallel hybrid vehicle will be higher because of the additional weight, at about an average of 16 horsepower. The gasoline engine will then be operating at 20 percent of its peak horsepower rather than 15 percent for the conventional vehicle. There will be a slight improvement in engine efficiency to maybe 22 percent at the higher load. In stop and go driving conditions, the overall system efficiency with brake regeneration will be about 26 percent. At times when peak horsepower of 100 is required, energy is drawn from the batteries to assist the gas engine. The energy stored in the batteries is essentially free as it has been collected and stored there through brake regeneration.

The conventional 2500 lb. car with its 115 horsepower engine will get an average of 34 mpg (city/highway combined). On the parallel hybrid, the system efficiency is increased to 26 percent from 20 percent, and the fuel economy would be increased to 44 mpg. But because the vehicle increased in mass by 7 percent, then fuel economy is also decreased accordingly to 41 mpg. I'm sure to get arguments with these numbers. The details are not important here, just the concepts; efficiency is improved because the engine is operated on average nearer its peak capacity. Consequently the benefit of the hybridization strategy is about 20 percent in this case; pretty impressive. Now the combined city/highway number published by Honda is 48 mpg, not the 41mpg I show here. How does Honda gain the other 20 percent?

Hybridization is not the only modification made to the Civic to increase fuel economy. There are three other significant strategies that can be employed to make improvements in fuel economy. All of these strategies involve lowering the work required to operate the vehicle. The first is in the vehicle aerodynamics, it does not appear the Civic hybrid has an advantage in this area vs. the conventional Civic. The second area is to make the vehicle lighter in weight; this is difficult with a hybrid that has to carry batteries and the motor in addition to the standard drivetrain components. Even with using lighter weight materials, the Civic hybrid is 200 lbs heavier. The third area is to dramatically reduce the rolling resistance of the tires. Using low rolling resistance tires, the average power requirement even with the heavier hybrid is reduced to about 13 hp. This reduction results in the additional 7 miles per gallon. This seems high, because the benefit is also a 20 percent improvement in fuel economy. The same benefit as hybridization.

This brings up a key point: there are many strategies to improve fuel economy that do not include the hybridization of vehicles. And these other methods are usually more significant. The biggest of those is weight reduction!

Now this begs the question: if significant fuel economy improvements can be made with low rolling resistance tires, why don't automakers install them on all vehicles? The answer is: low rolling resistance tires compromise tire performance in all areas. Ride quality is diminished, handling performance is diminished and braking performance is also diminished. I suppose the auto makers believe customers who purchase hybrid vehicles are more focused on fuel economy than on these other vehicle qualities. Another point I'd like to make: as in this case, usually when fuel economy is improved, safety is compromised. Higher fuel economy cars are less safe; this is true for hybrids too.

Prius

The Toyota Prius uses a more optimum strategy. The engine, instead of being operated at 20 percent of peak horsepower, is operated closer to 50 percent. Then the overall efficiency of the system approaches 30 percent. Combined fuel economy is about 50 mpg instead of the 48 of the Civic hybrid. In this strategy, a smaller gas engine is employed of 70 hp and a larger electric motor is employed of 44hp. When there is energy in the batteries and the vehicle does not require more than the 44 horsepower available from the electric motor, the gasoline engine is shut off and the vehicle is driven in electric mode only. When the batteries begin to get depleted, the engine is run at or above 50 percent of peak power. Power not required to power the vehicle is diverted to a generator to charge the batteries. Now a vehicle of this configuration will require the addition of another generator. Weight is about 2800 pounds by the use of lightweight materials in the vehicle.

Comparing the Prius to the Toyota Echo, the fuel economy on the highway test cycle is the same for both at 45 mpg. The city test cycle shows an improvement with the Prius to 52 over the Echo's 34 mpg. This illustrates a parallel hybrid only has an advantage over a conventional vehicle when opportunities for brake regeneration exist (opportunities to recover kinetic energy) as on the city test cycle, driving with frequent stops. In fact, if the Echo had low rolling resistance tires as the Prius does; the Echo would get 41 mpg city and 54 highway for a combined 46 mpg. So the actual improvement in fuel economy with the hybrid is only 4 mpg combined or less than 10 percent. In fact, in highway driving with all things being equal (low rolling resistance tires on both vehicles), fuel economy is worse for the heavier hybrid.

"Now wait a minute, the Civic had an improvement of 20 percent and you call the Prius strategy more optimum?" Here's a dirty little secret about the Civic. Lighter materials were used on the Civic hybrid to keep its weight at only 200 lbs more than the standard Civic. The Echo is about 2100 lbs, almost 700 lighter than the Prius. A non-hybrid Civic with the lightweight parts used on the Civic hybrid would similarly be lighter. As a result, much of the improvement attributed to hybridization on the Civic, should actually be attributed to weight loss. There really isn't a 20 percent benefit to hybridization on a 2500 lb car. The actual benefit of hybridization on the Civic is more in line with the Prius and is less than 10 percent. A 20 percent benefit could be realized on a vehicle weighing over 5000 lbs, such as a Dodge Durango. The heavier vehicle has more kinetic energy; so more energy can be recovered through brake regeneration.

A heavy hybrid

I know this is obvious, but I'm sure someone will ask. If heavier cars have more kinetic energy, then wouldn't a heavier hybrid get better gas mileage than a lighter one? No. The heavier car's engine converts a lot more energy to work to create the kinetic energy in the first place. It is true; a larger amount of kinetic energy is recovered and stored in the batteries. So a 20 percent improvement in fuel economy can be realized. A 20 percent improvement on a Durango which gets 15 mpg is only 18 mpg. If you really "care" about fuel economy, buy a lighter SUV, and you will get better than 18. **Weight savings are more significant in improving fuel economy** than making a car a hybrid.

EPA tests

The EPA tests for vehicle fuel economy consist of the city and highway driving cycles. When these numbers are published, this note is always attached; "Based on 2003 mileage estimates. Use for comparison purposes only. Actual mileage may vary." Usually actual mileage is worse, because actual driving conditions are more severe than these tests.

The city test cycle is similar to an urban commute to work without rush hour traffic. On this cycle the vehicle frequently is accelerated to speeds of about 30 mph and then makes 18 stops. The longest stop is for maybe 30 seconds. The Prius does excellent on this test, 52 mpg, as numerous opportunities to recover kinetic energy through brake regeneration are available. The Civic hybrid which weighs about the same does nearly as well at 46 mpg. With its smaller motor and manual transmission, it does not recover as much of the kinetic energy as the Prius. The Prius' more optimum strategy is illustrated on this test.

The highway test cycle is similar to a commute to work from a suburb freeway entrance ramp to a downtown exit ramp in mild rush hour traffic. There are no stops, but maybe three rapid decelerations which could provide a little brake regeneration. Often people think the highway test cycle is similar to taking a cross country trip. It is not. The average speed on this test is only 48 miles per hour. The Prius with the extra weight of its motor and batteries and the advantage of low rolling resistance tires is able to match the performance on this test cycle of the Echo at 45 mpg. The Prius engine is operated more efficiently than the Echo's to accomplish this. The Civic hybrid does slightly better at 51 mpg on this test. This is because the manual transmission on the Civic is more efficient in addition to the benefit of low rolling resistance tires and reduced weight materials.

Now the 10 percent improvement on making the Prius a hybrid is on the combined city/highway test. On just the highway test, all things being equal (aerodynamics, weight and low rolling resistance tires), the hybrid gets 17 percent worse fuel economy. On the city test only, the hybrid gets 26 percent better fuel economy for the net 9 percent improvement of the combined tests. The Civic strategy is not tilted so strong towards the city test and the numbers are about 10 percent worse on highway and 17 percent improvement on the city for a net 7 percent improvement.

Driving in the real world

If your driving habits are like those of the city test cycle, you get a 27 percent (the Prius) improvement in fuel economy as discussed with a hybrid. If you do highway driving, and want to get the best fuel economy, save yourself some money and buy an Echo. Don't take a trip with a hybrid; it's like packing an extra suitcase full of lead. At 65 mph, the Echo will use less gas than either hybrid. At 65 miles per hour, the Echo's engine will be as efficient as the hybrid's. With 700 lbs less weight, less work is required and better fuel economy results. At the lighter power requirements of 48 mph on the EPA highway test, the hybrids are only comparable because of the benefits of lightweight materials and low rolling resistance tires.

The reality is; hybrids only improve fuel economy when you are making frequent stops. Hybrids need stops to recover kinetic energy. If no stops are made, kinetic energy is lost in tire friction, aerodynamic friction, etc. The hybrid is heavier with batteries and an extra motor. More work must be done to propel it. If frequent stops are made, then some of the kinetic energy which was created by the more work done is recovered and later reused and improvements in fuel economy are achieved.

Most owners of hybrids graduated from a much larger car to their hybrid because of environmentalist guilt. I suspect these owners of hybrids are wealthy "elites." They wouldn't consider owning an economy car such as the Toyota Echo, so they would never compare the fuel economy of an Echo to a Prius. An actress, who was a guest on Letterman, told of her experience with a hybrid; it got better fuel economy than her Porsche. And you got to drive it in the carpool lane without having a passenger. It gets worse fuel economy in the carpool lane than a non-hybrid; no stops are being made! Even in conditions where the hybrid gets worse fuel economy than an equivalent non-hybrid, it still does better than a Porsche!

Let's compare a hybrid to a Porsche. A Porsche is a high performance sports car. It is probably the same weight as a hybrid. It has an engine that will make at least twice the power at say 200 hp. It has very grippy tires with high rolling resistance. If you drive it in average driving conditions like the city/highway test cycles, it will require maybe 18 hp on average, only 9 percent of the available power. Efficiency on the Porsche's engine at this power level may be as low as only 10 percent; this is why it gets such poor fuel economy. But the car can go over 150 miles per hour whereas the hybrid will probably only go 80 miles per hour.

Tips for hybrid owners

Don't take a trip from Phoenix to Flagstaff, Arizona. Hybrids don't like long hills. Your batteries will go dead on the first hill out of town and then the hybrid will be a gutless wonder as you climb to over 7000 ft in Flagstaff. With the extra weight of the dead batteries, fuel economy will be much worse than the Echo.

Don't turn on your air conditioning, your stereo or rear window defogger. These things take power. A/C takes about 3 hp to operate. Referring back to the standard Civic; with the air conditioning on, the engine has to produce an average of 18 horsepower (20 percent more). Fuel economy suffers because more work is required. Engine efficiency is slightly improved so fuel economy is only 10 or 15 percent worse. On the heavier hybrid, 13 of the 16 horsepower produced are used to create the kinetic energy which is later recovered when the vehicle stops. The additional 3 hp to power the A/C is never recovered. Because the engine is already downsized for better efficiency, the additional work to power the A/C does not have a significant effect on improving the efficiency over the non-hybrid engine. Fuel economy on the hybrid will be reduced by 15-20 percent. The benefit of a hybrid then diminishes a little more.

The big payoff for a hybrid is in city driving. Don't you all love "stop and go" driving? I know this is my favorite kind of driving! Not! So in deciding whether to buy a hybrid, you must carefully evaluate your driving conditions. If you are not constantly moving your foot between the gas and brake pedal every other minute; a hybrid will get worse fuel economy than an equivalent non-hybrid! Hybrids only have an advantage when you are doing driving where you make a lot of stops. Race car drivers like to go fast and turn left; **hybrid drivers like to go and stop, go and stop…!**

Insight

I have discussed how the Civic and Prius hybrids benefited from hybridization. I compared them to non-hybrid vehicles that are very similar. Now the Honda Insight is the best mileage hybrid available. How is it accomplished? The Honda Insight doesn't have anything you could call a non hybrid equivalent, except perhaps a motorcycle. It only carries two passengers. So it is difficult from the available information to determine the exact benefit from the hybridization of this car. However the advertised numbers for the vehicle add credibility to the simulation work in which I was involved.

The vehicle weighs less than 2000 pounds (this was Chrysler's goal for a 70 mpg hybrid). And the fuel economy rating is approaching 70 miles per gallon at a combined 64 mpg rating. As I have previously stated, there are three areas in vehicle design which can be addressed to improve fuel economy. The Insight has made great strides in all of these areas. Weight is less than 2000 lbs. Low rolling resistance tires are used. Though they do not publish the aerodynamics, it is apparent significant reductions of aerodynamic drag have been accomplished with the Insight design. On the Prius hybrid, the benefit from hybridization was a less than 10 percent fuel economy improvement. If that same benefit were to be applied in the case of the Insight, a non-hybrid Insight would get 58 mpg.

The benefit of hybridization is proportional to the kinetic energy available for brake regeneration (remember, heavier vehicles benefit more from hybridization). When less kinetic energy is available (via a lighter vehicle), this energy cannot be recovered as efficiently. As a consequence, the benefit of hybridization on a lighter vehicle like the Insight will be smaller than on the heavier Civic or Prius. Our computer models were showing only a 5 percent increase in fuel economy on a 2000 lb. car. This would indicate a non-hybrid Insight would get about 61 mpg combined. The hybridization benefit is therefore only 3 mpg. So justification for a hybrid Insight that cost $18,500 ($2,000 tax credit included) over a non-hybrid Insight that could sell for maybe $12,000 is a much tougher sell than in the case of the Civic.

Now consider real world driving conditions with the Insight; running the A/C and driving on the highway. In these conditions, there may not be any benefit to carrying around some heavy batteries and electric motor. The Insight gets super high mileage primarily because it is a tiny "piece of crap" car! If Honda really cared about saving gas, they would offer a non-hybrid Insight at much less money. They don't though, so what is their goal with such an offering?

I recently had a conversation with the junior Senator from Utah. He owns a Honda Insight and drives it around Washington DC. He reported to me he was getting an average of 53 miles per gallon. This is 7 percent lower than the advertised rating of 57 mpg for the CVT version (I don't know which version he has). Perhaps this is due to operation of the AC. He is considering trading it in for a Prius, noting the annoyance of the Insight being a tiny two seater. Now I'm speculating, but if an Insight were without the extra weight of its batteries and electric motor, it would probably get better than 53 mpg when you drove it around running all of your accessories. That's low tech, who would want one of those?

Ford hybrid

In the 2002 Annual Report, Ford plans to offer a hybrid Escape SUV in 2004 as a 2005 model. They call this hybrid system, "split hybrid architecture." It is very similar to the Toyota system and should result in the same benefit.

I recall reviewing a patent that had been issued several decades ago for a unique new type of automatic transmission. A conventional engine was attached to a planetary gear set; the gear ratio was controlled by an electric motor attached to different gears in the gear set, thus creating a CVT (continuously variable transmission). The reason you never saw a vehicle with this type of transmission until now is because it required an electric motor and batteries for it to function, thus requiring the added expense of a hybrid vehicle. Remember most inventions are usually a stupider way to do something that is already done. The Ford hybrid will now cost how much more, and get 20 percent better fuel economy? Remember that a portion of that 20 percent is actually due to weight reduction and/or low rolling resistance tires.

Chapter 22

HYBRID NONSENSE

Saving the Planet

Hybrid vehicles are expensive. Essentially it is a car with 2 engines, a more complicated transmission, more computer controls, likely an extra generator and some expensive batteries. It probably costs more than twice as much to manufacture vs. a conventional vehicle.

A Toyota Prius brochure asks, "how far will you go to save the planet?" It then answers, "about 566 miles per tank." You're impressed with this and you've decided you're willing to compromise the safety of yourself and your family and do your part to save the planet. Like *Billy Cruiser* (the two foot driver), you like pushing on the pedals a lot! You're a "go and stop" man! You're ready to buy a hybrid. Does it make sense?

Honda offers the Insight starting at $19,080. EPA mileage estimates are over 60 mpg, not far from Al Gore's vision of up to 80 mpg. It weighs less than 2000 pounds and will carry one passenger in addition to the driver. After sales tax and fees and with the federal income tax credit of $2000, you will probably have invested $18,500 to buy your 65 mpg car. Alternatively you could have bought a Toyota Echo which gets about 39 miles per gallon, with the total investment of about $12,000; a difference of $6500. You live in a market where gas prices are two dollars a gallon. You Drive 12,000 miles a year. By spending the extra $6500 dollars, you save $246 dollars a year on gasoline. In 26 years you will save $6500 dollars in fuel costs and the Insight will have been a more economical investment than the Toyota Echo.

Now if you lived in Europe and gasoline is $5 a gallon, you would save over $615 a year on gasoline and would recoup the $6500 in just over ten years. Now that makes a little more sense. I used the Toyota Echo in this comparison because it is the highest mileage non-diesel powered car offered on the market. The Insight is the best hybrid scenario. But if you were to compare an Echo to the Prius (comparable size), then the hybrid is even less sensible. In fact both have a highway mpg rating of 45.

Now I am married and I have a few kids, so the Insight is not the car for me. I'm going to buy a Prius or a Civic hybrid. I opt for the Civic, I like

Hondas better. After licenses and taxes and my $2000 income tax credit, I'm into my Civic hybrid $19,000. I could have gotten a Civic DX for about $14,000 after taxes and licenses. But it only gets highway mileage of 38 mpg, whereas my Civic hybrid gets 51 mpg. I drive my car 15,000 miles a year. With gas at 2 dollars a gallon, I'm saving $202 a year on gasoline by buying the Civic hybrid for $5000 more. In 25 years, my $5000 investment will have paid off.

My wife's brother-in-law claims his calling in life as an educator keeps him so busy he has no time for recreation. His life is just work and rest to get ready to work again. Important people (elites) like him don't have time for recreation. For someone like this, a vehicle is just transportation to and from work. However for us that don't have such a high calling in life, someone like me who is a motorized recreationalist, a vehicle is more than just transportation to work. In and of itself it can be a toy. In my case, I need a vehicle to tow the trailer that contains my other toys. Though a few Americans are like my wife's brother-in-law, the majority is probably more like me and has time for recreation. "Damn Capitalism!"

Hybrids are only useful as commuter cars, and have very limited capability when it comes time for recreation. Don't take one on a trip, you'll likely burn up all the gas you saved in the last year of city driving. I suppose this is why you don't see people standing in line at the dealerships to buy hybrid vehicles. It seems they are mostly sold to those who have a higher calling in life (the elite), so they can arrive at the Oscars in one and "look" like they care about the environment.

The reality is hybrids are really just a toy for these wealthy folks. Most the time they will be in their much safer limos or their big SUV with tinted windows. At the last event where I encountered the Senator from Utah, he mentioned he needed more "Detroit iron" around him to make his trip to St. George, Utah and was driving a big Mercury. After all, hybrids are just tiny "piece of crap" cars with a big price tag. I'd like to see one with an odometer reading over 10,000 miles. People that buy 'em, don't drive 'em!

Now there are always exceptions. The junior Senator from Utah has got over 15,000 miles on his. He does play with his toys. This wealthy elite walks the talk, that's kind of why I like him.

100 mile per gallon carburetor

Often when I am sharing the stories about hybrids among my family and friends, I am told about the 100 miles per gallon carburetor (electric cars do the equivalent of this). I am told of how the oil companies in conspiracy with the automakers bought the patent for this technology and never allowed the carburetor to be produced. But this is an old wives tale.

When my grandfather died on a fishing trip out in Nevada, we drove a 1968 Plymouth Fury III with a 383 V-8 the whole way drafting behind a semi truck and got nearly 30 miles to the gallon. Normally this car was lucky to get 12 miles to the gallon. The point is; dramatic alterations in your driving habits can make a significant difference in the fuel economy of a car. But with typical driving habits; (I'm being negative here) a car getting 100 miles per gallon is physically impossible. It is simple physics: gasoline only can be converted to energy at a maximum of about 30 percent efficiency, and the work to move the car doesn't change a whole lot. In my example of drafting behind a semi truck, the work required to move the car was dramatically reduced. This is how improved fuel economy was achieved.

Despite the old wives tale, in the back of Popular Mechanics magazine you could find someone that would sell you a conversion kit for just such a carburetor. My older brother ordered one of these. In the instructions included with the kit, it used the example of the fuel efficiency of a locomotive pulling a freight train (a locomotive is actually a series hybrid without batteries, so only 3 energy conversions). I don't know if you've ever ridden on a freight train or not, but they take about 20 miles to accelerate to their cruising speed. In order to achieve improved fuel economy, you were instructed to have driving habits similar to that of a locomotive pulling a freight train (don't accelerate fast). Additionally the instructions explained that much fuel was wasted in heating up the engine. So a device was included in the kit for heating the engine from your electrical socket of your home. It also instructed you to not start measuring your fuel economy until you were sure that the engine was fully heated to operating temperature. You were instructed to over inflate your tires to reduce rolling resistance. My brother didn't finish this project; I don't blame him.

Additional Energy

As with the hundred mile per gallon carburetor example and the drafting behind a semi truck example, dramatically improved fuel economy was accomplished by severely altering driving habits. Energy was also borrowed from other sources (wall outlet or semi-truck drafting) to provide some improvement in economy. In the case of hybrid vehicles, there is also a little bit of this going on. Let me give you some additional thoughts about considering the actual energy you save by driving a hybrid vehicle.

Back in 1998, the Toyota Prius went on sale in Japan. Auto makers from around the world flocked to Japan to buy them up, so they could study the Toyota hybrid technology. The Chrysler cost estimators estimated it cost $40,000 to manufacture the Prius. Compare this to the manufacturing cost for a Dodge Neon which at the time was about \$10,000. The Toyota hybrid was a pretty good deal for \$20,000. Well it takes energy to manufacture a car. In the case of the Dodge Neon; imagine the energy that is expended to manufacture a \$10,000 car. Raw materials are mined out of the earth, energy is expended to form these raw materials into parts and these parts are transported to the assembly plant. Now imagine the energy expended to manufacture a \$40,000 hybrid car, made out of more exotic materials. Do you think it would require more or less energy to manufacture than the \$10,000 car? I don't really have a good idea myself, as we didn't do any studies of this type. I certainly do believe more energy is expended to manufacture a hybrid. If more energy is expended to manufacture a car that uses less energy; is the result a net use of more or less energy? Are we just robbing Peter to pay Paul?

Stupid

Think back on the "Smarter Engineer" principal which I learned from Bob Bachelor. Hybrids are STUPID! Not because they deliver impressive fuel economy, but because they are so damned expensive! You get the function of a \$10,000 "shitbox" car for \$18,000 so you can save \$200 a year on gas. Any thinking person would call that "stupid." They only improve fuel economy in unpleasant driving conditions.

"Oh, but I'm saving gas for future generations." you whine. If you care so much about saving gas thinking you're saving the planet, buy a house closer to your work or get a motorcycle that gets 100 mpg, you hypocrite! Any place where driving a hybrid would save gas (meaning you stop and go a lot), public transportation is available and would save even more. Or really make an improvement and kill yourself taking a car off the road permanently. Sorry for my rant, but all those who cry "save the planet" never do anything about it themselves. They just try to impose restrictions on everyone else to force them to do it.

The press loves hybrids. It is because the press is full of a bunch of liberals that voted for Al Gore, and they think the internal combustion engine is evil! They write articles which praise the virtues of hybrids. But they don't apply any reason to their reporting, because they want you to buy hybrids (they can't afford them or refuse to ride around in a little "piece of crap" car, but think you should).

One article opened by saying "hybrids usually get over 60 mpg." Only 1 does and only 1 version of it! What does the word "usually" mean to this dolt! Another headline reads, "Autos make big switch from electric to hybrid." What does "big switch" mean to you? I would think it would mean a big chunk of models would be offered as hybrids. Only three are offered!

No wonder the press has little credibility! They corrupt our language for their politics. A headline on a recent opinion piece reads, "Hybrid cars are step toward fuel-free dream." This guy should get a pedal car. He thinks "alternative fuel" means "fuel-free"! Dolt!

Buy a hybrid

Now that I have dissed hybrids, I'll give you a reason to buy one. Back to my definition of "Reliability"; a hybrid will have an increased driving range if you stop a lot. Thus you fill the gas tank less often, less "interruptions in its intended function" and reliability is better. Buy a hybrid, it's more reliable.

Will people buy hybrids? Yes. American Motors learned there is a market for "Weird" cars. They would sell 100,000 Gremlins the first year it was introduced, and then sales would plummet. They had the same experience with the Pacer. The theory went: there is, in our population, a group of people that buy cars that are different because they want to be different. Thus people that buy weird cars. My dad bought Vegas and Citations (these weren't weird, just crappy); there are people that buy the crap no matter what it is. Unfortunately weird car buyers are a minority, and don't buy a new one every year. I can see this group of buyers buying hybrids. There are a few that still want to buy electric cars even as stupid an idea as they are. Heck, if enough of this book sells, I'll buy a hybrid just to demonstrate my theories presented here!

Stupider buyers

You probably assume most people think logically when purchasing a car. This is not so, thus I introduce you to the "The Stupider Buyer." I know "stupider" is not a word, but I'm using it here. The wealthier a car buyer is, the less he considers when purchasing a vehicle. I'm sure formal research would bear this out, but this is a conclusion I arrived at by my own personal interactions with wealthy people. I asked one wealthy gentleman I was acquainted with if he would be interested in certain features on a Grand Cherokee if they were offered (he was a current Grand Cherokee owner). He responded, he would just ask for the most expensive one and be done with it. When you're rich, it is a badge of honor that you spent more for yours than he did for his; thus the "stupider buyer." Remember the dealer telling us they were losing sales of Grand Wagoneers to Range Rovers because the Range Rover was the most expensive SUV at the time. So perhaps rich people will buy hybrids just because they cost more!

Honda, Toyota and Nissan were not ignorant of this concept. In the highly profitable decade of the 80's, many yuppies had become wealthy by making wise decisions like buying economy cars that were a good value. But with this new wealth, they wanted to serve their vanity by being a stupider buyer. They had previously bought Hondas, Toyotas and Nissans. But these companies didn't have any really overpriced cars. So these buyers turned to Europe and bought over priced Mercedes and BMWs. The Japanese solved this by creating their own lines of overpriced cars. These are Acura (Honda), Lexus (Toyota) and Infiniti (Nissan). Now vanity could be served from across the Pacific too.

Vehicle pricing

Chrysler cost estimators pegged the cost of a Prius at nearly $40,000 to manufacture. I doubt the number is really this high, but be assured it is more than what they sell the car for. One always jokes when you are losing money on a sell; that you need to make up for it with volume. Sometimes this can be true, as a larger volume wholesale buy can result in discounts where you can actually turn a profit. However I doubt Toyota can totally make up for this on the Prius. So it is in Toyota's financial interest to keep sales down. Kind of like when the good news at AMC was that Alliance car sales were down.

Now you're a reasonable person; you ask, "Why would Toyota or Honda sell a car at a loss?" Most automakers do actually sell some models at a loss, usually the entry level models. They do this hoping to build brand loyalty and sell you a more expensive model later. Selling hybrids is the same; they are seeking to build brand loyalty among the "granola" crowd. A vehicle's price has nothing to do with the cost of manufacturing it. The price is determined by market research which indicates how much someone will pay for it. Perhaps in the early days of the industry this was not true, but it is the reality today.

Cars built on assembly lines in North America cost anywhere from about 10 to 20 thousand dollars to manufacture. Most sell for more than $20,000. So you see this is a very profitable business to be in. Some economy cars however, are sold for less than the manufacturing costs at about $10,000. Fortunately, these are only a small percentage of sales.

You will notice the most expensive cars only cost twice as much to manufacture as the cheapest. The most expensive models often sell for more than twice as much, thus they are highly profitable for the automakers. I remember the premium Grand Cherokee sold for around $35,000 and only cost about $13,000 to manufacture. The base model Wrangler cost about $10,000 dollars to manufacture, and sold for about $14,000. The lessons here: the manufacturing costs are only slightly higher for more luxurious models. Manufacturers make a lot more money on the higher line models!

Now I can assure you hybrids cost more than $20,000 to manufacture. Market research at Honda and Toyota revealed people were not willing to pay much more than $20,000 for them (after all, they are only tiny "piece of crap" cars). So that's what they sell them for. They hope that these vehicles will build their image as an environmentally friendly company, but prefer that you spend your money on a Sequoia or Pilot SUV where they can put a lot of cash in the bank.

Caring

Among those who have the view that automakers don't care about the environment, the offering of hybrid vehicles is an appeasement to them. Both Toyota and Honda and soon Ford are able to lay claim they "care" about the environment. This makes for good publicity among the "Granola" crowd.

The majority of this crowd when confronted with the sticker shock of buying a hybrid will opt for a non hybrid model. Nevertheless they will feel good about their decision, because all of their friends will buy the hybrid from the same car company. And the car company will breathe a sigh of relief, because they didn't lose money on a sell.

Politically, offering hybrids has already been able to stave off additional regulation from the federal government. Both Toyota and Honda are now offering much more profitable sport utility vehicles, and additional regulations would have made it less profitable for these companies to expand their lineup with larger vehicles. It also detracts from the profits of the American automakers, as they must spend money on research into the same foolishness. Government Regulators can point at Honda and Toyota and say, "See, they can do it, why can't you?"

In the Toyota literature I looked up on the Internet, they brag there are over 100,000 Prius hybrids on the road. With success like that, you would be expecting the hybrid system to be offered on other Toyota models. They do not really want to sell more. However, to keep their "green" image up, they have announced an upgrade to their hybrid. I suppose with the dollars lost on each one sold, they can only afford to subsidize sales of about 20,000 vehicles a year.

Now that I have demonstrated the foolishness of hybrids, I will get back to my experience at designing them with the Chrysler HEV program

Chapter 23

GOVERNMENT BRILLIANCE

The government HEV program

Chrysler signed a contract with the DOE; they were now partners with the DOE and with General Motors and Ford to develop hybrid electric vehicle technology. What this entailed was frequent meetings with all the partners. About every other month we had "sharing" meetings. Preparation for these meetings usually involved how to look like we were sharing something when in fact we were not. We never really wanted to let GM and Ford and even much less let the government know what we were working on. But it was a nice opportunity to associate with our peers at the other two companies. And, in fact, after the presentations, there were informal deals made and some information was shared.

To tap into the "brilliance" of those in academia and to use the ingenuity of the brightest that were studying in their universities, the "Future Car Challenge" competition was organized. Cars which included the Intrepid, Lumina, and Taurus were given to several Universities to be converted to 80 mpg hybrids. I suppose the DOE expected them to show us the way. As I had become a part of the HEV team, I was selected as an industry judge along with many of my peers for the competition. The competition was to have a meet once a year and go for three years.

In the first year, it was my opinion the school that did the best had not yet converted their vehicle to a hybrid. It was a Chevrolet Lumina simply with the gas engine replaced by a VW TDI diesel. It got around 44 miles to the gallon. I wasn't surprised, as my computer model also showed this configuration had some promise. However this really had the people from the DOE upset, because this did not demonstrate the validity of the DOE belief that a hybrid would be superior. With the goal of getting up to 80 miles per gallon, who is thinking outside the box when the only acceptable answer is "hybrid?"

NREL, our contract administrator, was located in Golden, Colorado. Monthly meetings were held with the NREL personnel. Because the NREL personnel only involved two or three people, and the Chrysler personnel was a larger contingent, these monthly meetings were usually held in Detroit. Except Steve Spencer was an avid skier, so one of these meetings would be scheduled in Colorado during the winter and usually on Thursday, so a vacation day could be taken on Friday to go skiing. Chrysler would pick up half the tab for the airline tickets and the DOE would pick up the other half. I went on one of these trips and spent my vacation day skiing with my boss. I was wishing I was on a snowmobile.

The aluminum Taurus

In addition to research being done on the hybridization of vehicles, research was being carried out at some of the national laboratories on lighter weight materials, improved aerodynamics and ways to lower tire rolling resistance for vehicles. Meetings were held where information from this research was shared with us in the industry.

Ford built a small number of Taurus models which were made with aluminum bodies. One of the laboratories had been given one of these aluminum bodied cars to evaluate the effect of the lighter car on fuel economy. This is why you don't give projects to the government: After a year they reported they believed there was an improvement in fuel economy, but their testing method was inconclusive.

The aluminum Taurus was placed in their fleet of pool vehicles. Pool cars could only be used for official company business and not after hours (official lab policy). There was not another Taurus in the fleet. Consequently, the vehicle was rarely driven in rush hour traffic. The fuel economy was closely monitored. An employee at the Lab owned a comparable Taurus with a steel body, and commuted each day in rush hour traffic. This vehicle was used as the baseline since there was not another Taurus in the fleet. The fuel economy was better than the baseline, but the comparison was not valid considering the very different conditions in which the two vehicles were driven! "Duh!" that was me sitting at a table during the presentation with my jaw dropped. Then the presenter continued, "But to get more valid results we have decided that we will try to get permission to violate the lab policy on pool vehicles and have this employee use the vehicle for his daily commute. Then our conclusions will be more valid." You couldn't have thought of that a year ago? This was very typical stuff at these meetings; I usually tried to get out of them. Eskelson Principle #2 (the idiots get hired by the government) deftly demonstrated here.

Notice the nature of this "government" research project. They evaluated the effect of an experiment by Ford. They didn't do their own experiment. And you know for sure that Ford already knew the effect on fuel economy of the lightweight body! The government evaluation was a year late and bungled! This is typical of the government labs.

Everyone tried to get out of these meetings, although we were under at least an implied obligation to have people attend. I occasionally could not get out of attending. I attended another one in Washington DC, and the only thing I remember was the multiple overtime playoff hockey game on the TV that night in which I stayed up until 2 am to watch until the end. When the Red Wings finally scored, the entire hotel erupted. Everyone else there was from Detroit too. I suppose all these meetings help out the hotel business. A lot of money is spent to travel to these fancy places where we are told, "Our conclusions could be more valid if we had done things more intelligently."

Dim Smore and Al Gore

Because *Dim Smore* was such an integral part of Al Gore's vision, he was invited to Mr. Gore's home near Washington DC. Actually it was a reception for many who were working on the supercar project. But even *Dim Smore* with his own huge ego, was impressed to be in the home of the Vice President. He took up a large chunk of time in a staff meeting to tell us about it.

Intrepid ESX showcar

Shortly after the contract had been signed with the Department of Energy, a show car was in the plans for the Detroit auto show in 1996. Originally it was to wet the publics appetite for the redesigned 1998 Dodge Intrepid. Suddenly the showcar was to have a hybrid drivetrain. It was known as the Dodge ESX.

I think Mr. *Smore* volunteered us for the task. Research with the DOE contract did not provide enough to stroke his ego. This would put him in front of spotlights. There was much complaining, particularly since we had no direction in the hybrid program. Mr. *Smore* promised we would provide a functioning drivetrain for the vehicle. Luckily because I was still new to hybrids and simulation, I was just an observer on this project. The auto show was such a short time away; there was no time to study different hybrid alternatives.

As previously stated, the simplest hybrid is a series hybrid. Since this would be "easy" to do, it was the design direction established for the ESX show car. A "Gen Set" powered by a small diesel engine would be added to the drivetrain from an electric minivan. Two wheel motors were used at each front wheel instead of one and drive shafts like on the minivan. This was the "Liberty Way", promise we had technology, and then scramble to invent it.

Even this early in the program, we knew a series hybrid would not be the direction for the Chrysler HEV program. Nonetheless, the ESX showcar was to be a series hybrid, building what we knew was obsolete hardware would waste our time leading up to the show. We made-up impressive fuel economy numbers (lies) that were slightly based on our simulation.

After the Detroit auto show in January, press rides in the car were held for several months/years following. We didn't actually deliver a hybrid drivetrain. On these rides the vehicle was driven as an electric vehicle, with the diesel engine operated for the sound effects. The scheduling of press people to drive the car was done to insure the batteries would not be depleted (only a few at a time, then it was put back on a charger before the next group). The diesel engine and generator controls to charge the batteries had not yet been developed. All show and no go! At least it wasn't a pushcar.

With the impressive promises made with the ESX and the silence from GM and Ford (they didn't have the Liberty Way), the ESX garnered quite a bit of attention from the press. Steve Harding and Bob *Leery*, who did the majority of the work on getting the vehicle ready to show, were interviewed often. It seemed they really enjoyed the attention. The press was told fuel economy would be in excess of 50 miles per gallon. Our simulation showed about 30 mpg. We couldn't really test for fuel economy, because it wasn't really a hybrid. Truthfully, it was an **electric car with a diesel engine noisemaker!** Bob would occasionally wonder about the lies he would tell and weigh the morality of it against the fawning of the press which he clearly enjoyed.

I've read many stories by reporters who have driven the vehicle. Rarely do they mention the diesel engine was even started. They think they are driving a hybrid, but in fact they are only driving an electric car. They'd been duped!

Chapter 24

THE CHRYSLER HYBRID

The real program

Despite Liberty's focus on the ESX show car and the time wasted with stroking the DOE people's egos, the real HEV program did start to evolve. The simulation model progressed to the point we had confidence in the predicted performance it indicated. In fact we were getting close to the Government's goal of 80 mpg and came up with a vehicle that had a predicted mpg combined of 72. I have noticed Chrysler still publishes this number as the number for the now future ESX III. This sounds pretty impressive. But it was produced with flawed assumptions.

To accomplish 72 mpg, the vehicle was configured as follows. It could seat five people (same as the Dodge Intrepid). It had a test weight of 2000 lbs with a driver (in cyber space). The aerodynamics or CD (coefficient of drag) was .19. It had low rolling resistance tires. It used a 1.2 liter diesel engine. The electric motor was rated at about 20 hp and also operated as a generator for brake regeneration. Coordinating the diesel and electric motor was an automatically shifted manual transmission. Nearly every aspect of the configuration uses some bold assumptions which I might dare say are impossible to achieve. I will discuss each.

For the vehicle to achieve a test weight of 2000 lbs, the actual weight needed to be 1850 lbs to account for an average driver. The Honda Insight which only seats two meets this target. We obtained a Neon made out of aluminum during the project as a test mule and its weight in a hybrid configuration was in excess of 2000 lbs. Diesel engines have higher combustion pressures than gasoline engines, and thus require stronger materials in their manufacture. VW has a 1.9 liter turbo diesel that is extremely efficient and meets US standards for emissions. Diesels as I mentioned, normally require stronger materials, thus are heavier, making the weight issue even more difficult. VW's diesel powered cars weigh about the same as the two heavier Japanese hybrids, several hundred pounds heavier than the gasoline powered VWs. I am not saying it's impossible to build a diesel engine hybrid that weighs 1850 lbs the size of the Dodge Intrepid. But you won't do it with just the body made out of aluminum. It will require even lighter materials, perhaps one we commonly know as "unobtainium." Talk about an expensive car to build!

A CD of .19 was the best achieved on any vehicle in the world at the time. The 2004 Prius is .26. The Insight may be close. But there is not yet a 5 person car that has achieved this. Not impossible, but a very tall order for the designers.

And we assumed improvements in low rolling resistance tires. Remember with less rolling resistance, you get less traction and thus less safety. Not to mention the harsher ride.

In our computer model, we used VW efficiency scaled down to our 1.2 liter diesel engine. We approached our diesel engine supplier and asked they develop a 1.2 liter diesel. Our management had assumed this was simple to do. Well this isn't so simple. The VW TDI diesel is a 4 cylinder and is therefore 4.75 liters per cylinder. We were informed when cylinder size is smaller than this, as in the case of a 3 or 4 cylinder 1.2 liter diesel, that efficiency is compromised. This is due to the size of the orifices in the injectors which cannot be made smaller because of the molecular size of the molecules in diesel fuel. A 2-cylinder diesel requires extraordinary measures to control engine shake and therefore efficiency is also compromised. But *Dim Smore* would not hear any of this negative talk and we continued to use the flawed data in our computer model. A 1.5 liter 3 cylinder diesel was used on subsequent mules and show cars.

The automatically shifted manual transmission had not been developed yet. It takes work (energy), usually by a human driver to release the clutch and operate the shift lever on a regular manual transmission. Likely this is a small amount of energy, nevertheless our model made no account for the energy to do it automatically.

The electric motor was sufficient to supplement the power of the diesel, and was more efficient at converting energy in the regenerative braking events than a larger one. So we called it a mild hybrid or "Mybrid." By the way, this is very similar to the Honda hybrid strategy.

Dim Smore when confronted with these flaws backed off on telling the press we could get 72 mpg with the hybrid but promised 70 mpg. Apparently he saved the 72 number for the ESX III. The ESX II show car would demonstrate this technology for the 1998 Detroit Auto Show. Again we promised a demonstration of technology which did not exist. Unlike the series hybrid of the first ESX which could be driven as an electric vehicle, the parallel hybrid configuration could not. The vehicle was driven on diesel power most often. Not many in the press got to drive this one, smoke and mirrors could not be utilized to hide its flaws.

Suppliers

Part of the HEV contract was to select companies to supply the components. Ultimately Chrysler selected Delphi (their parent company is General Motors) as the supplier for the hybrid vehicle electric motor. So if the General Motors HEV contract was not enough corporate welfare for them, they got a good chunk of the Chrysler contract to boot.

Chrysler doesn't build diesel engines, or batteries, and as I have pointed out they don't make electric motors either. So the only thing Chrysler does build for a potential hybrid vehicle is the body. All of the major components similar to the electric motor which was sourced to Delphi were sourced to other companies which specialized in their own areas of expertise. This, in many circumstances, is actually a smarter way to do business. But it has its drawbacks too; often you can't get exactly what you want, and you get the leftover technology. Certainly the best technology at Delphi is reserved for the GM program.

Benefit of hybridization

As I discussed in my evaluation of the Honda Insight, the benefit of hybridization to the Chrysler hybrid is about five percent. The Honda Insight shows a combined 64 mpg rating, just 6 mpg (10%) less than our diesel simulation of a hybrid. The Honda uses a gasoline engine with a peak efficiency of 30 percent; our hybrid uses a diesel engine which has a peak efficiency of 40 percent. This accounts for the 10 percent difference. With a hybridization benefit of only five percent, a non-hybrid vehicle, meeting all of our other goals would get fuel economy of 66 mpg combined. This vehicle without all the batteries and the electric motor could more realistically meet the weight goal and could be manufactured cheaply enough that perhaps it could be sold at a profit.

With this knowledge, the program didn't make much sense to me. I suggested it might make more sense to make a hybrid out of a Durango, because a 20 percent improvement in fuel economy could be realized on something that massive. As had been my hallmark throughout my career, when we were pursuing something that looked ridiculous to me, I let them know. Remember, my criticism of the F1 Grand Cherokee landed me this job here at Liberty. The forces that dictated it be a hybrid were much bigger in this case. It was going to be a hybrid, because those in the government wanted a hybrid. And "the government knows what's best."

I thought the goal was to improve vehicle fuel economy and lessen our dependence on foreign oil. Instead it was to stroke the egos of a bunch of bureaucrats who believed the answer was "hybrid." I was working with a *Dee Lusion* again. Because of my history of telling the truth and speaking my mind, the others in the department made sure I never spoke to the press. This entailed making sure I was never working on support of the show cars.

Bent nails

Once I was sitting in church, and the speaker told this story: "My Father worked in construction, and when I was quite young he would occasionally take me with him to his jobsite. He gave me a bucket filled with bent nails. He showed me how to straighten the nails with a hammer and then directed me to straighten the nails. I noticed that he never used these nails I had straightened and I became curious and asked him why. He said once a nail had been bent, that it was weaker and would easily be bent again." He then praised his father for teaching him the value of hard work as this story illustrated.

But to me, the story looked like a father was just keeping a little kid busy so he wouldn't be bothered while working. If I'm given a task that doesn't seem to accomplish anything except to keep me busy, such as straightening bent nails; I can't stay motivated to keep doing it. When I share this story, I get lots of arguments: Such as there is a higher purpose I don't understand, or it helps you develop a work ethic. However with my small mind, if I can't see the purpose in my work, I'm not motivated. I suppose those with more faith than me can stay motivated.

I had been doing hybrid research for three years; hybrid vehicles no longer made sense to me. All this trouble for an economy increase of five percent only if you drive it the right way (stop and go driving). I no longer could stay motivated to work on the program.

Previously, in my performance review in December 1996, Mr. Spencer, as with my other managers throughout my career, was impressed with my technical expertise. He also praised me for learning to do simulation. However, he wanted to see more motivation out of me. I made a conscience effort throughout the year. In my performance review of December 1997, he noted the improvement in my behavior (I had straightened a lot of nails for him). My performance review also reflected this improvement. But shortly after the performance review, the foolishness of the hybrid program became so dominant in my thinking that I could no longer keep up the charade. This was stupid!

Chapter 25

EXIT STRATEGIES

Adding to the simulation team

After we (I) had started the simulation work, there were still many holes in it that needed improvement. Bob *Leery* was making no contribution as he spent most of his energy on being an "engineer celebrity" and showing off the ESX to the press. I was not producing results as quickly as desired. We got approval to hire someone to help me. Primarily we were looking for a new college grad that had some experience in the MatLab/SimuLink software. We interviewed several candidates, and only two or three impressed me and I did have a favorite. My favorite was not Bob's, and Bob persuaded me to go with his favorite.

I will not name the guy. He was not any help. He screwed up the computer model on many occasions. I would spend hours trouble shooting just to figure out what he had screwed up. After this happened a few times, I made sure he never messed with my version, so it wouldn't get screwed up. I had enough to do without someone with "Flame Like" intelligence providing me more work. I occasionally fed him my latest model after he screwed up the one he had. Kind of like giving him some "bent nails" to straighten.

At first we attributed this to him being inexperienced. However it became apparent to me after several months he would never gain enough competence to actually make any contribution to the team. Bob did not disagree with me; nevertheless he did not want to take any action (like firing him and getting some actual help). Bob felt if we let him go, it would make us (him) look bad. It was our first excursion into the finding and hiring of personnel. If we let the guy go, it would indicate we didn't do a very good job. So I just did my best to stay away from him and not let him screw my work up. He was not even a direct hire. See, it's hard to get fired from Chrysler no matter what!

Simulation hardware

We used standard PC's with Windows to do our simulation. This was slow as we were using Pentium computers with speeds of 33 MHz. As our model got more complicated, it would take several hours to do a simulation run. Faster computers (133 MHz) were available and we asked if we could get these. Our request was granted and we got 66 MHz Pentium computers. This helped some. Nevertheless I questioned why a big corporation like ours, doing important work on a government program with important people like *Dim Smore* leading us; could do no better than getting newly obsolete hardware. I was granted a designer workstation with a 200 MHz processor and that speeded things up a bit. This was inconvenient as it did not have Windows and we had to learn a little programming. Finally when Intel introduced 200 MHz processors, we got 166 MHz Pentium computers and they performed more to my expectations. For my home I went out and bought a 200. Why couldn't Chrysler?

Other options

One nice thing about working in the auto industry and a benefit of the unions (we always got the same holidays that the union negotiated) was the number of holidays we got. We never worked the days between Christmas and New Years. In December 1997, I flew to Arizona to visit my sister. I told her about how disillusioned I had become with the hybrid program at Chrysler. Since this had been my dream job, I wasn't sure what my future with the Corporation would be. She offered me an option, "Why don't you quit and come help us build our new house this summer."

When I went back to the office in January, my motivation fell off a cliff. I could not motivate myself to work on simulation anymore. I spent most of the time in the office playing solitaire on the computer. At some moments I questioned my own sanity. I made an appointment with a Psychiatrist through Chrysler's health care referral network. This Doctor after listening to me for about an hour; told me I was the one normal person at the asylum. She didn't think I needed to do anything except get out. It was my only visit.

I got called into *Dim Smore's* office. He had an idea (I think that it was the *Environmentally Sensitive Hybrid Vehicle*) on a "new" twist of the hybrid configuration. He explained it to me, so I could do a simulation of it. I asked him what answer he wanted. He said, "72 miles per gallon." Right there without doing any simulation I said, "There's your answer!" I don't recall if he ever spoke to me again. Nevertheless that's the number he used to brag about the performance of the configuration!

I had a conversation with Steve Spencer and indicated I wanted to find another position at Chrysler. He empathized with my frustrations and indicated he might leave before I did. He asked I continue to work on the simulation until I leave. I told him I would, however I couldn't keep this promise. I could never find the motivation.

I looked for another position for a couple of months, but could not get interviews for positions I thought I could be interested in. The positions I did get interviews for, I didn't find interesting. Being a Liberty employee is kind of like getting AIDS, once you've got it, you're stuck with it. A fellow Liberty employee once compared owning a Bayliner boat to AIDS also; it seemed that owners of those could never get rid of them either. Rarely did any employee leave Liberty for another position in the company, reinforcing my observation that it was a holding tank for the corporation's misfits. After being sent to Liberty, it seemed everyone else in the corporation knew I was a misfit and only those with crappy positions showed any interest in having me.

Around the end of March, I decided to put my house up for sale. When it sold, I would resign and move to Arizona to help my sister build her home. I told Steve and he said he understood my feelings, and wished me good luck.

Repercussions

Now when I stopped doing simulation, simulation stopped. Until I stopped, it appeared the simulation team, Bob *Leery*, the nail straightener and I was getting a lot done. Bob took much of the credit. When the work stopped, it made Bob and the other look like they didn't do anything. Bob particularly was upset with me. He started the process to get me fired. It is possible to get fired from Chrysler, but it takes at least a year. I was gone by August.

The process to get fired is thus: An interim performance review is conducted where the subject employee is given some short term goals to accomplish in the next 2 or 3 months. If the employee does not meet these goals, then adverse action can be taken. Usually he will be put on probation and another performance review will be given 2 or 3 months later when action will then be taken if no improvement is shown. Now this technically can happen in less than a year. But it takes at least a year for the person in management to get up the courage to do the process. Bob actually did not have the authority to give me a performance review. Those with the authority weren't so anxious to deal with me; probably because I would confront them with their own incompetence. So he attempted to get me to start the process myself. Bob kept asking me to make up goals for my interim performance review (like I didn't know what an interim performance review was for), and I kept telling him I was working on it.

Until I left, I was not totally useless. The ESX II show car had some severe engine mount problems. I didn't have much experience with engine mounts and nobody else at Liberty did either, perhaps this is why it was such a problem. I quickly found some experts. Experts are always anxious to share their expertise; it validates their value. The Liberty philosophy was if an expert was consulted, it would box in our thinking and the best design would not be done. We always could think outside the box and always knew better and therefore we didn't ask any experts. Consequently every design done was laughable! Fortunately for the ESX II, I applied Eskelson's "principle #3." I figured someone was more expert than me and my experience was they would be more than happy to help me. I used their advice and we quickly had good engine mounts. With this done, I went back to playing Solitaire.

Steve Spencer left to become an executive engineer on one of the vehicle lines. His replacement was Gerry Gardiner. His experience was in automotive electronics. Probably a good fit since a lot of electronic control systems would be required on a hybrid. I reported to Gerry for about a month, then the organization was changed and the chassis work was given to *Dim Wiser*. I actually sent my resignation letter to him. The merger with Daimler-Benz had been announced.

To encourage employees to patent their inventions and as an incentive to invent, Chrysler would pay a bonus of $1000 to each employee named on the patent. This occurred when the patent application was accepted by the patent office. Chrysler would own the patent. Inventing things was part of our job, so our only reward was the bonus and a pretty plaque for our wall. This is why I did not contest *Dee Lusion* being on my suspension patent, as my bonus was still $1000. In fact I had one of the designer's name added to the patent so he would get the bonus too (this was kind of a mild protest for *Lusion*'s name being on the patent).

Two patents for hybrid vehicles had been submitted which I was party to. Though I was anxious to resign, I feared I would forfeit these bonuses by doing so. If I had sold my house, I would have resigned risking forfeiture of the bonuses, but my house hadn't sold yet. Before Steve Spencer left, he had asked for my resignation, but I declined offering these reasons. He said I would still receive the patent bonuses; however, I didn't trust him at that point and didn't want to take the chance. I have since learned my name was on an additional patent which was filed after my resignation. I'm still waiting for that check.

In April, I had taken a load of my things west to store at my father's house in Utah. In June I had turned in my company lease vehicle and had purchased a ¾ ton '82 Ford truck. The truck was really ugly (different colored body parts with rust) and I took pleasure in parking it among all the new Chrysler products in the lot at Liberty. It was a subtle way of giving them the finger. I had scheduled 2 weeks vacation at the end of July. I emptied my house into my ugly truck and onto my snowmobile trailer and headed west for my vacation. I figured I'd return and work until my house sold or I received the patent bonus money. In my paycheck at the end of July was the patent money. I couldn't bring myself to go back. I stayed in Arizona and sent my resignation letter to *Dim Wiser*. My house sold in October and I have not been back since.

Not over yet

You'd think after Chrysler received my resignation, they would leave me alone. Some years earlier, Chrysler bean counters came up with a scheme to save the corporation money. It would only affect employees when they quit. Before the scheme, you worked a year to earn vacation and then took that vacation the following year. If an employee quit, the corporation then paid them for the vacation days they had not yet taken. The scheme went that you forfeited one year of vacation and then took vacation in the same year you earned it. If you never quit, you would never notice. Your failure to resign when the plan was announced was your acceptance of it. Well, I had taken more vacation than I had earned, so I had to pay them some several hundred dollars back. They threatened me with legal action and I complied even though I disagreed.

Many at Liberty were worried I would write a book. I didn't think much about them and helped my sister build her home. I didn't have ill feelings toward them as many of them may have assumed. My dream job was to do research and development at a big car company. I finally achieved my dream and it was a joke. The pay was good. I haven't quite figured out what to do with the rest of my life. Maybe I'll write a book!

Part 6

POLITICS, THE FUTURE
AND CONCLUSIONS

Now that I've told you my stories, I'm going to give you a few of my
opinions.

Chapter 26

POLITICS

Conservative vs. Liberal

While living in Michigan, I was an engineer. As the years passed, I became more and more interested in politics. The trigger for my participating actively in politics had to do with boating access issues. Increasingly, access to waterways in Michigan with personal watercraft (PWCs) came under assault. Also my career was greatly affected by politics, particularly when I worked on hybrid vehicles. Not only did I go to the polls and vote in every election, I started attending public hearings and voiced my opinions. I also wrote letters to state representatives, US Congressmen and Senators.

Back in the 1992 presidential primaries, I bought the mainstream press garbage and went through a stage of being an Al Gore supporter. I briefly was a supporter of Bill Clinton and eventually helped him get elected by voting for Ross Perot. When I say mainstream press garbage, I mean the Liberal agenda which said George Bush didn't care about anything but Foreign Policy. This was the constant pounding by TV anchors and local papers.

One of the Detroit papers would publish a voting guide before each election. Candidate's responses to questions were printed regarding all the races in question. After reading through this, I nearly always voted for the Republican candidate. When I did vote for a Democrat, it was usually because the Republican's responses sounded the same as the Democrat's. Though I didn't label myself then, I am a conservative, and Republicans are conservative more often than Democrats. Often Republicans are not very conservative, so often my vote for them is because they are the lesser evil.

When John Engler defeated an incumbent Democrat by just a few votes to become Michigan's Governor, I was proud I voted for him. In 1994, I went to the primary to see that Spencer Abraham became the Senate Candidate for the Republicans. I thought Ronna Romney (former RNC chairperson) too liberal and too much of a socialite to represent me in Washington. I was ecstatic when Abraham won (I didn't think a Republican could win in

Michigan). Now I've left Michigan and they defeated Abraham and have a Democrat Governor. Does one person make such a difference?

When I say I'm a "Conservative," this means I'm pretty content with the way things are and I don't want change. "Liberal" means things are not very good, and so things need to be fixed (not that liberals ever fix anything, then they'd have to turn conservative). At times in our country, both philosophies can play a positive role in providing greater freedom. I am conservative because I like things the way they are. Sometimes laws are needed to keep things the way they are, so conservatives do pass laws.

Gridlock

Though I nearly always voted for Republicans, I didn't like them getting new laws passed either. It seemed that whenever any new laws were passed, that we lost a little freedom. I don't feel any politician, Republican or Democrat, is competent enough to pass legislation that improves things. The news media portrayed "gridlock" as a negative thing. I thought it was wonderful! If any politician could promise gridlock, they would have my vote. I often told friends and relatives that "Gridlock is a good thing!"

When the government shut down under Clinton, It was great. For that time, wasteful spending stopped, and we didn't lose any freedoms. Now that power has tilted to the Republicans nationally, more freedoms have been lost in the name of the "new tone" than we lost with eight years of Slick Willy. I hear many prominent conservatives say how grateful they are Bush is President. If Gore had become president, there would be gridlock for sure. We might still have kept some freedoms that have been lost with Bush as our President. Do you think Republicans in the House and Senate would have ever sent a Campaign Finance Reform bill to Gore? Not likely!

I have real mixed feelings with Bush as President. I am pleased with tax cuts and the success in the war on terrorism. I am pleased with his administration's actions on Public Lands issues. Such as keeping snowmobile access in Yellowstone. But on the other hand, I long for days of gridlock when no freedoms were being taken away. If he would just veto something, anything, just to show he will keep a campaign promise; I might quit looking for an alternative to him. I am sincerely afraid he's going to only serve 4 years like his dad. He needs to show Republicans he is a Republican.

Mainstream Media

In 1992, I had been duped by the mainstream media into voting for Ross Perot, thus helping Clinton become president. After watching Clinton bumble along and observing the press worship him, the bias towards liberalism in the press became glaringly obvious to me. Detroit's NPR station had become the first choice on my dial before Clinton. After their soft treatment of Slick Willy, I started to turn them off when they quit playing music. I didn't trust the mainstream media to tell me the truth.

I joined some conservative organizations, and relied on their publications to get accurate information. I had heard of Rush Limbaugh through the mainstream media. He was portrayed as a right wing kook and I thought the right wing media as bad as the left (I was still being duped). As the most popular radio talk show host, I figured he could only rise to this position with the blessing of those in power. I never made an effort to listen to him.

Shortly before leaving Michigan, a friend lent me one of his books on audiotape. I agreed with everything he said. Still I didn't listen to his radio show. When I arrived in Arizona to help my sister build her house, she suggested I listen to Rush while I worked. "He's quite entertaining and he says many of the same things you say." Well I tuned in, and I've been a Rush listener ever since. He explains it better than I can. He hasn't changed my political views, he's a conservative too. I just understand them better, because he explains them better than I can.

Utopia

Men through the ages have dreamed of a perfect society. A "Utopia," you might say. Can such a thing exist? According to Bob Bachelor's principle, "Perfection is the Enemy of Good," such a society wouldn't be very good.

In my religion, a perfect society called the "United Order" was tried early after the church's organization. It wasn't very good. In the United Order, a member voluntarily gave all his property to the church and then only took what he needed. Each member was to use their skills to work for the Order. Well, as you can imagine, some members thought other members were not doing enough. Others thought others took more than they needed. Bad feelings were rampant and it became very contentious. It failed and the church lost many members who felt ripped off and some who were upset because they could no longer freeload. After the failure of this "perfect" society, the church then asked members to volunteer 10 percent of their earnings as "tithing" to support the church. With this less than perfect method, the church has grown and has done much good since.

Socialism is very similar to the United Order. Except in socialism, your property is confiscated, not voluntarily given. And someone "wiser" than you decides how much you need. If men were perfect, socialism might work. But men are not perfect, so socialism always fails. It doesn't motivate people to work. When great wealth already exists, socialism seems to work for awhile. But gradually, it removes the motivation for productivity and results in equal poverty for all, except for the "wiser" ones.

In America we have Capitalism. If you work harder than your neighbor, you can have more. So inequalities arise. If you don't work, you will starve. So everyone is motivated to produce at some level. Is it any wonder this nation produces so much? Our poor people are fat. How poor can they really be? In socialist countries, the poor are emaciated. It is not perfect, but Capitalism is "good" because it motivates everyone.

Some other nations have copied Capitalism, always with great success. Think of Germany and Japan. After WWII, we set them up like us, and they churned out riches. Now they have adopted many socialist policies, and their riches are shrinking.

It's better there

I often hear Liberals say how much better it is over in Denmark and Sweden. The citizens are taken care of from cradle to grave as I understand. My most prominent ancestry comes from these two places, but I am not anxious to immigrate back!

When I think of Denmark, my first thought is it is a haven for perverts and junkies with legalized prostitution and marijuana. Many children, girls and boys, are forced into the trade. How does the state take care of them? The stories I've read do not give me the impression much is done to protect these victims. So who are the people the state cares for? Whenever a liberal acquaintance spews the virtues of Denmark, my thoughts go out to those oppressed by the enlightened socialist society there.

While in Detroit I had a friend who was a native of Sweden. He loves America, because of the freedom he enjoys. He later became a citizen because he loves this country so much. He went out and bought two Personal watercraft. He noted in his native Sweden, he couldn't just go out and buy PWCs. First of all, he wouldn't be able to afford them, because the government taxed him so heavily. And if he could, he would have to show a business reason to justify the purchase (rental operator or racer). You can't just get one for the fun of it. In these socialist countries, these pleasures are only for the noble and elite. Here, any ordinary Joe with a little ambition can enjoy a PWC.

Soda pop conspiracy

On a few occasions in my life, I have visited other countries. I've been to Japan, France, England and Canada. While working in France, I remember wanting a candy bar. There were only four choices in the vending machine. This prompted thoughts of how great we have it here in the U.S. We have usually at least 20 or more choices in our vending machines. Like with PWCs, we just have so many more choices. With all these choices, you would think you could find a really good soda pop.

When I was a kid, I used to walk down to the corner gas station and get a bottle of soda pop. My favorite was "Orange Crush." It actually had pulp floating in the bottle. It had so much flavor; I loved it. I don't remember when it happened, but it was before I got my drivers license; Orange Crush changed. It no longer had any pulp and tasted like orange colored 7-UP. There were other flavors I loved too, which also changed and tasted like colored 7-UP. The only tasty soda pop seemed to be colas. I didn't drink much soda after that. I assumed at the time, the flavor was taken out to lower the quality of the product to increase profits.

In my early 20's, I visited Japan. There I got Fanta orange soda. It had flavor that harkened back to the Orange Crush I had loved as a kid. Then, when in France, again I got orange soda that had pulp in it. So my question is, as great as America is, why can't I buy a decent orange soda here?

I've thought about this a lot. I've come up with a theory I call the "soda pop conspiracy." Coke and Pepsi have bought up all these small soda pop companies like Crush and have watered down the flavors so the only decent tasting pop is cola. Cola is addictive; therefore we drink more pop if we drink a cola. Thus, all other soda flavors are designed to entice us to drink colas. I suppose if you wanted to drink a really great soda pop everyday, and did not ever care to own a PWC, living in Sweden or Denmark might be better than living here.

Coke and Pepsi have monopolized the soda market and we no longer enjoy the choices we once enjoyed. Here is a valid function for government; to break up such a monopoly so we can enjoy choices in soda. Will some politician please break this monopoly, so I can enjoy a great orange soda here in the USA. He would have my support.

Exploitation

It is the nature of man, to exploit others. Slavery is the most graphic example of this. Many less severe occurrences are a part of this nation's history. In fact it was the exploitation of the first American settlers by England that led to our fight for independence. Our constitution grants us individual rights, so we as citizens can resist being exploited. Notice it does not end exploitation, but gives us power to end it if we choose. Not a perfect system, however a good one.

The "Elite" in the world who desire to exploit others find this frustrating. It is their desire to destroy these rights so they can exploit others to acquire the wealth and position they believe they deserve. Our Constitution has been under assault since its ratification. The brilliance of it is; it still survives some 200 plus years later. I observe in our nation three kinds of people: those that love our Constitution and love this great land, the elites that hate the same and the suckers who believe the elites.

At times through our nation's history, both "conservatives" and "liberals" have fought to end the exploitation of people. Today, there is very little exploitation occurring in our great nation. We have more freedom than has ever been enjoyed in the history of the world. Similarly, the elites are working harder than ever to take freedom away.

Technology and freedom

Why do we enjoy more freedom today than 40 years ago when there were no emission standards on cars? Or 100 years ago when there were no speed limit signs? Not only do we have the freedom granted by our constitution, even though somewhat eroded, it is because of technology that we have even more freedom!

Before Henry Ford put a car in every house, most in this country could not move about easily. It was horses or public transportation, neither of which was very swift or convenient. The automobile has given the population the freedom to live where they want, work where they want and access to goods and services like never before. If you are being exploited at your job, you can quit and easily drive to a better one. Today with computers, and cell phones, we access information instantly. This makes our freedom even greater. Though many different technologies have expanded our freedom, I think the automobile is the most significant.

Government regulation

I have mentioned in the book, the stupidity of the government's involvement in the design of hybrid vehicles. The U.S. government is very heavily involved in the auto industry. And politics directs government policy. That is why it gets a chapter here in a book about cars.

The auto industry is heavily subsidized by the government. Cars need roads to drive on. The automakers do not build these roads. Governments build the roads. Therefore the transportation system of this nation is a joint venture between the government and the automakers. The increased freedom we enjoy because of the automobile is not only a result of the industry; it is also a result of the roads our governments have built.

Because automakers have this dependency, they have responsibilities

to these entities that build roads. Automakers have skirted these responsibilities whenever they could. It was correct in my view for the government to establish and enforce <u>reasonable</u> emission standards; pollution
had become severe and a fix was needed. The automakers would not clean
up emissions (it would cut into their profits), and the government needed
to force them. This is where "liberalism" played a positive role in our
freedom, assuming I have correctly assigned the origination of emission
standards to liberals.

Of course when these standards go beyond reason, it hurts the automakers and hurts our freedom. My point is; regulation is justified because
the industry is so heavily subsidized, but it should be kept reasonable as to
insure the health of the industry and our nation. The cooperation between
the government and industry has brought us the great freedom the automobile provides. President Bush's policies seem more reasonable than the
idiocy that had spawned from the Clinton/Gore era. I had been a part of
that idiocy.

Freedom haters

I have mentioned there are elite in our society that hate freedom and
seek to destroy it. The elites are a minority, so they cannot tell you directly
what they desire. In the past when it was easy to exploit people, they dis-
guised themselves as conservatives and resisted change, so they could
continue the exploitation of others. In today's society, they have changed
their disguise. Freedoms need to be taken away for them to be able to effectively exploit others as they desire. So now they are liberals. They come
in many different strips; activists, protestors, environmentalists, etc. Under
this guise, they go about their work.

The automobile is good for our society. These elites call it evil. Elites
have you believe they dream of a day when we can travel and not pollute.
In reality their dream is of a day when only they can travel. Al Gore is no
dummy; if he can eliminate the internal combustion engine, he can control
the movement of the people. No wonder he would have you believe the
internal combustion engine is a bigger threat to nations than any war machine.

First the elites attacked cars as gas guzzlers in the seventies and predicted we would run out of oil. The only reason we now have trouble getting oil, is they employ every tactic they can to stop us from drilling for it.
So we go to other countries where the leaders exploit the people and the
land to get oil for us. Then they accuse us of dealing with despots and being dependent on foreign oil.

For awhile, we bought the rhetoric and little economy cars were the norm. We didn't run out of oil. There are more reserves now than there was then. So we have started buying big gas guzzlers again. Now they are called SUVs. They're attempts to label them "evil" with the "gas guzzler" moniker doesn't work this time around. So now they are "dangerous monsters." Now "SUVs are killing people." The truth is; highway deaths are down compared to when economy cars were the norm. Nowadays, with more cars on the road than ever before and with a bunch of them being SUVs, there should be more deaths on the highways than ever. Why isn't there?

These efforts at calling these certain types of vehicles "evil" is really only an attempt to take away freedom! **The only reason we have shortages of oil, is because we bow to those who want to take away our freedom!**

In the West, they are trying to close as many of our roads as possible. With the vastness of the land, westerners have often improvised when it comes to roads. It can be prohibitive to construct roads and occasionally we have used dry creek beds as roads. The elites come out and claim these are not roads and close them. So not only are they trying to eliminate cars, they are trying to eliminate the roads too. Both are assaults on our freedom!

Most liberals and environmentalists are Democrats. Some are even Republicans. A Republican Senator driving a hybrid? I work hard to elect conservative Republicans when they really are, because I love freedom and my country!

Chapter 27

THE FUTURE

Hybrid Vehicles

The hybrid vehicle programs among the US automakers originated with Al Gore's promotion. Al Gore is the chief of those that would like to eliminate the industry. Do you believe the purpose of these programs was to help the auto industry? It may have contributed to the end of Chrysler with the takeover by Daimler. Hybrid vehicles are a joke. They only get better fuel economy in unpleasant driving conditions. However, wherever they could make an impact in reducing energy use, mass transit is available. Using mass transit would reduce energy use even more. So they just don't make sense.

Toyota and Honda are building hybrids. No one else is. The American automakers keep announcing plans to build them, but haven't yet. In the liberal havens in Europe, no manufacturers have even made such announcements. It is rare that Japanese Automakers take the lead in new technology. Usually they copy someone else and make it a lot better. Why were they the first to market with hybrids? Let me tell you a little about the Japanese so you can understand why.

Let me take you back to the "bent nails" story. The Japanese are very hard working. You give them a task and they will usually execute it better than anyone else. Though they seem to do this well, they give little thought to what the task accomplishes. This is the case with the hybrid. They believed a hybrid was what our market would demand, because the liberals in this country said so. They gave no consideration to whether it really did any good or not. I lived in Japan for two years. This scenario is totally believable.

Hybrids are an example of Liberalism exported. The idea of a hybrid originated here. It was touted as the bridge between gasoline cars and the future when the internal combustion engine would be eliminated. The Japanese embraced it and ran. Now they make some really expensive little cars that nobody wants. An auto dealer I know says many of them are showing up at the auctions and go unsold.

The hype about hybrids will continue, but I find it unlikely you will ever have to use the fingers on more than one hand to count the number of models available.

Fuel Cells

I don't see hybrid vehicles ever gaining widespread acceptance in the market. We can't afford them, and the automakers can't afford to sell them. While surfing the net I read a quote by Daimler-Chrysler executives that hybrid vehicles would not be built in significant volumes unless US customers accept their higher costs. Chrysler does have some intelligence at the top after all. Electric cars have been abandoned. Environmentalists have now pinned their hope on the fuel cell.

The fuel cell does have some promise. Fuel cells combine hydrogen and oxygen to create electricity. I have mentioned a lightweight car requires about 100 hp when accelerating. And then to cruise, only 15 to 20 hp is required. Fuel cells are not able to make such rapid changes in power production. And a 100 hp fuel cell is likely to large for a car. So a fuel cell vehicle is essentially a series hybrid vehicle with the fuel cell replacing the engine and generator. The fuel cell will produce about 30 hp and the excess will be stored in batteries for periods where excess of 30 hp is required.

It is reported that some fuel cell vehicles are starting to appear on the roads for testing. The first hydrogen filling station has been installed in Iceland. It is reported that these cars will travel about 100 miles between fill ups. This sounds like an electric car and thus will not be as <u>reliable</u> as a gas powered car. Hydrogen only has 25 percent of the energy per gallon of that of gasoline. So range could be an issue with fuel cells. But a 100 mile range this soon in the research does show promise. I won't be holding my breath though.

Alternative Fuel Vehicles

There are currently vehicles powered by compressed natural gas (CNG) and some powered by different forms of alcohol. These alternatives work well and often pollute less than gasoline powered cars. However, similar to hydrogen, these fuels do not have as much energy as in a gallon of gasoline. Alcohol has about 50 percent of the energy compared to gasoline. Efficiency is comparable to gasoline engines. Thus, cars powered by these alternative fuels are not as reliable. They require much larger gas tanks or more frequent refueling. Until gas supplies disappear, acceptance of such vehicles will be small.

Need for a New Generation Vehicle?

Engineers in the example of Gerry Hennesy always believe that things can be improved. However, just because it is "new" or "different" does not mean it is improved. Do we really need a "new" generation of vehicles?

The internal combustion engine has powered cars now for over 100 years. The reliability is incredible. New car emissions have become so small that on a smoggy day, the air out the tail pipe is cleaner than the air going in. If a better technology can be developed to power cars, wouldn't it have come along by now? Will fuel cell cars ever be as reliable as gasoline powered cars? Will we run out of oil? I believe that it is not an accident gasoline has been the primary fuel source for cars for more than 100 years. Perhaps there is not a need for a "New Generation Vehicle!"

In this book, I made references to things I deem miraculous. A "miracle" has reference to Deity; therefore, one could conclude I believe in God. It seems the common belief in the world is; "science and a belief in God are in conflict." Many churches in the world preach things that insult common sense and the practice of science. One example is a church that does not allow for blood transfusions of their members. So in the science of medicine, they are denied the blessings of the miracle in healing the procedure provides. Hence, there is conflict between their religion and science. It is not an accident I used the word "religion" instead of "God" in describing this conflict. I do not believe there is a conflict between God and science. I have read at various times, that Albert Einstein did not find this a conflict either.

Most religions describe God as "All Knowing", and that would make him the "Ultimate Scientist." Science is the pursuit of knowledge and the utilization of such knowledge. Thus the "Great Scientist" will inspire men and teach them to do great things. I believe God has inspired the many inventions that expand our freedom and will inspire many more to come. I view them as miraculous. Is it possible, that gasoline with its energy density is just the best way in the universe to power a car? Could it be the "Ultimate Scientist" has taught us this knowledge and we have been refining it for 100 years? I'll make a bold prediction; the internal combustion engine won't be replaced in my lifetime.

Before I leave the subject of God, I feel the need to talk a little about those who put down the miracles of God. These elites and liberals have decided these inventions God has inspired are "evil." Yet things that used to be called "evil" -- lying, cheating and immorality in general -- are now enlightened personal preferences. There are people that have had many millions of acres of land set aside for their religious experience, known as "wilderness". These elites are healthy and travel by foot into areas of nature where there are no Jeeps allowed, so they can "get close to God." We have the same experience when we travel there by Jeep, but they want to deny us that experience because we do not have the physical capability. I suppose they are more "enlightened."

Electric car idea

Though I have dissed alternative powered vehicles, there may be opportunities where they could be used to expand our freedom. Using my TRIZ training I came up with this idea regarding electric cars. I have espoused the virtues of electric cars, the fact that they put out zero emissions and are very energy efficient. But the "conflict" (TRIZ buzzword) is that they cannot store very much energy.

I doubt I alone have thought of this idea. As we do with electric commuter trains, we could have electric cars draw power from the road. I envision the carpool lanes in large cities that go largely unused be converted to electric vehicle lanes. A system would be designed so the electric cars draw electricity from the road to propel the car and charge the car's batteries. Then once out of the carpool lane, the batteries power the car to the job or house. As an incentive for people to buy electric vehicles, the power in the carpool lanes is provided for free. This could put a lot of electric vehicles on the road in large cities

Cleaner energy

With the electric carpool lanes in the previous paragraph, the energy to power these would currently come from a coal-fired generator out near a National Park; thus not putting out zero emissions. Nuclear power plants put out zero emissions, except when there is an accident like Chernobyl. But this accident in a third world country with antique technology pales in comparison to lives lost and the quality of lives deteriorated through the mining of coal. We need to move past "The China Syndrome" and build some new Nuclear power plants. And with new technologies, we can generate even more power with spent rods, thus solving the problem of nuclear waste. It seems such a waste that we as a country have become so scared of Nuclear Power. It's zero emissions power!

The future is bright

New styles will emerge, and gas will power them. Diesels might start to power more of them too. Diesel engines are more efficient, and with better fuels for them coming on the market, emissions are coming under control. More and more vehicles will be diesel powered.

If we run out of oil, we will make synthetic gasoline (alcohol) which may cost much more (maybe then hybrids will make sense). The energy density advantage will still make these cars the most reliable.

Chapter 28

INTELLIGENCE AND IDIOTS

Chrysler Success

Often I feel very insignificant in the world, I'm only one person. Do my efforts ever matter? While I was with Chrysler, they were very successful. I hardly believe I was the reason for their success.

Under the leadership of Bob Lutz and Francois Castaing, the engineering organizations were reorganized after the pattern of the AMC organization. They had the most attractive lineup ever in the history of the company. They forged relationships with suppliers that saved money and increased profits for both. They solved most of the problems their cars had with the competence of their engineers like me. They gave huge profit sharing bonuses to their employees, which brought loyalty. They were the low-cost producer in the world. Their success was held up as a model for the industry by the press. Other manufacturers studied and envied Chrysler.

Chrysler bragged they were spending less on research than similar sized companies. They thought this a virtue. Many eggheads in the world, who know more about these things than me, expressed corporations needed to spend about twice as much on research as Chrysler had been to stay competitive. And since Chrysler's research was actually used to facilitate the disposal of misfits; actual research dollars were really much less. With the advent of the PNGV by our liberal government friends, the few dollars still being spent on research were committed to the stupidity of a hybrid. With the government help, research essentially ground to a halt. Technologically, this was Chrysler's only flaw. A merger with Daimler solved this flaw. However, Chrysler still had the brain power to survive without the merger. Using Eskelson's "principle #3," sometimes it can be an advantage to be behind in technology; you can quickly copy those more advanced and catch up. Often with spending much less than the originators who were copied. Chrysler had become very successful and had the capacity to continue despite these weaknesses.

The merger

I am disappointed Chrysler merged with Daimler. I personally would have preferred Chrysler continue its tradition as one of the big three US automakers. I'm going to be an armchair quarterback here, and give my opinion to why the merger happened.

Often as an engineer, we spoke disparagingly of finance people, calling them "bean counters." Since leaving Chrysler, I have learned some things about finance and I have quite a bit more respect for bean counters now. When Lee Iacocca brought the corporation back from the brink of bankruptcy, he did it with great leadership and marketing skills and with the help of some great bean counters; Jerry Greenwald and Steve Miller. Lee's marketing skills convinced many Americans to buy the little "piece of crap" K-cars. Greenwald and Miller managed the money and Chrysler came back. Much of the profit was spent on diversification. Not an unwise thing to do in my opinion.

This is the point where Lee should have stepped down. He began to make mistakes. Lee figured with his "celebrity" he could get people to buy the inferior cars indefinitely. So little was invested on new vehicle designs; Americans got wise, and stopped buying the crap. By the late '80s, Iacocca had to rescue the corporation again. This time the fix was not as easy, because the buying public had grown much wiser. New higher quality products were needed. This is where the leadership of Bob Lutz came into play. By the mid-1990s, Chrysler probably had the most exciting product offerings of any automaker in the world. Times were good again.

Because of Iacocca's stubbornness in leaving, Chrysler lost its two best bean counters, Greenwald and Miller. Iacocca picked a car guy, Bob Eaton as his successor. As an engineer, it is romantic to me to have a "car guy" in charge of a car company. However, the realities of doing business in this world are such that a really good finance guy is needed at or near the top. With Eaton and Lutz in charge, there was a vacuum of this talent at the top.

Chrysler was again raking in the dough with their fabulous lineup. Now I'm a stupid engineer. I think saving money in the bank is a good thing to do. When the cash stops flowing, I'll just pull it out of the bank. This is fine for a private entity to do. But Chrysler is a public corporation. And when the biggest shareholder Kerkorian (a finance guy) sees $7 billion in a rainy day fund, he gets nervous. It's almost one third of the total value of the corporation. His logical next step is to make the corporation private to protect his investment. His plan to take the corporation private makes more sense to me than merging with Daimler.

I don't believe a bean counter like Greenwald or Miller would have ever put Chrysler in such a vulnerable position. Iacocca left the company in poor hands when he could have left it in good hands. Well there is nothing that can be done about it now. I'll just mourn a little bit.

Intelligence not required

For 11 ½ years I had a career I loved; I truly expected to retire from Chrysler. Until 6 months before I left, it never occurred to me to do anything else as a career. But I was not delusional, I had been sent to Liberty because I was shoved aside. I don't believe it was in the best interest of the corporation for me to be shoved aside. I was very talented and had done much which had benefited the corporation. I could have done a lot more.

I had discussions with many of the other misfits (we were all together at Liberty) about this phenomenon I now observed. One in particular predicted doom for the corporation because his expertise was not being utilized. Chrysler continued to be successful (if you call merging with Daimler success?). And this success was still going on without him and me. I concluded our intelligence was not required for the success of the corporation.

In a large corporation like Chrysler, the law of averages would indicate many on the staff would be idiots along with some smart ones. So the processes to design cars had been put in place to protect the corporation from the idiots. These processes can be frustrating to the competent. The result is; the cars get designed and manufactured. A lot of money is made. Most of the idiots get shoved aside. Some of the competent get shoved aside too, just because it is possible for it to happen. When you pull up the tares, some of the wheat gets pulled up too; but the harvest is still bountiful.

As Bob Bachelor taught, the smarter engineers do it for cheaper. Chrysler was the low cost producer in North America, so you could conclude they had the smartest engineers of any auto company. Nevertheless, other auto companies also have enormous profits. The net result of shoving someone as important as me aside and others like me is maybe that Chrysler is no longer the low cost producer. They will still make a lot of money.

If I hadn't have worked at Chrysler, things wouldn't really be very different. The problems I solved would have been solved by someone else; perhaps by consultants, which they would have had to pay much more than me. There are others in the world as smart as me, you know! Maybe they are smarter, because they get paid more for their services.

To build cars, it takes a lot of people. It used to bug me that Chrysler seemed to put a premium on those with an MBA. But this now makes sense to me. The biggest key for Chrysler to be successful is that many thousands of people be organized so cars can be produced. People that are expert at organizing a lot of people are of the most worth to them. There is a good supply of competent engineers, I've listed many I worked and associated with. However, organizers are harder to come by. Organizing people is not as much fun as engineering. I didn't want to do it!

Thinking back on the history of Chrysler; Walter Chrysler's genius was in manufacturing, or in organizing the assembly plants to be much more efficient. To design his first car, he went out and hired Zeder, Skelton and Breer. In fact their first design for Walter was a piece of crap; a technician on the project had to tell Walter (he couldn't figure it out himself?). They did a redesign and Chrysler organized a bunch of people to build it. As talented as Zeder, Skelton and Breer were; there is not a car company with their name. I am pretty sure they were better car guys than Walter. But Walter Chrysler organized people and got cars built! Better cars came and went. What it took to succeed was organizing the people, which Chrysler did!

Having the best product does not mean success. In fact rarely is the best product the most successful. Look at VCRs; VHS stomped on the superior Beta system. In computers, Windows dominates, where Apple is regarded by most to be superior. So success isn't the domain of the best and smartest. It seems to be the domain of those that work the hardest and are persistent.

Proliferation of idiots

The situation where Bob *Leery* and I hired the idiot, and then never got rid of him is unfortunately not an uncommon occurrence. This is one reason why there begins to be so many idiots working at large corporations. Strategies must be employed by such corporations so these idiots will not destroy them. In an ideal world, you would admit your mistake and fire them as soon as you recognized they were idiots. But to advance in a large corporation, admitting a mistake does not enhance your career opportunities.

Chrysler's strategy was to assign the idiots to do research, thus moving them aside so the work can get done. The idiots deluded themselves onto thinking they were doing something important, and were kept out of the way. In the short term this was effective. But the idiots took over the research and then research deteriorated into foolishness (like rubber band cars). Eventually the inmates are running the asylum. Research is essential for the long term health of a company. Chrysler used to brag they spent less on research than other similar size companies. Now they can brag their

CEO has a German accent! I can't tell you whether this was a deliberate strategy (assigning idiots to research) or if it just evolved from the circumstances. It did seem pretty consistent, though.

Al Gore's ideas were shoved aside too. The strategy was effective not just on people, but worked well when stupid ideas were rammed down the throat of Chrysler, like the PNGV. Just like the dolt that got assigned to do research and deluded himself he was doing something important: Al Gore and the DOE were deluded into thinking Chrysler was making a serious effort at meeting the PNGV goals. It appears this strategy was effectively employed to stroke those in the government into believing the automakers were serious about hybrids.

The effect of the PNGV program on Chrysler was useful research ground to a halt. Could this have been a strategy to weaken Chrysler by Al Gore (hater of internal combustion engines) and his cronies? Or is it just the natural unintended consequence of government "help?" Either way, government help usually isn't!

It seems other corporations have different strategies for dealing with the idiots. Another strategy I've heard of is that of Jack Welch, the CEO of GE: Every year they let go of the bottom 10 percent of their employees. That ought to get rid of some idiots!

The only other corporation I have experience with is General Motors. When I worked for them, my responsibilities occupied an average of 20 minutes a day. Now think about this: If I'm an idiot with only a tiny bit of work to do, perhaps I'm not such an idiot I can't do it, however miniscule it might be. Or I share my cubicle with someone else who is competent, but so bored they will do my job for me just to entertain themselves. In this situation, really competent people could be assigned to research. General Motors hasn't merged with anyone! They aren't the smartest by Bob Bachelor's standard. But as I mentioned early in the book, generally the smartest are not the most successful. I am personally an example.

I had been shoved aside and I knew it. Since I wasn't delusional about this, perhaps I am a bit smarter than the others who had been shoved aside. I didn't want to continue with a corporation that didn't want me! I had fun; it was my dream job. This is where I wish I wasn't so smart. If I was delusional, I could just keep hammering on the bent nails and be content. There I was, one of the experts in the world, doing what I used to only dream of, and it turned out to be a joke. Thank God I have the good sense to laugh!

The End

About The Author

The author worked in Chrysler Engineering for 12 years beginning in 1986 in the American Motors "Engineer in Training" program. He became an expert in vehicle alignment. Later he moved on to the team that did the early design of the 1997 Jeep Wrangler and the 1999 Grand Cherokee. His last three years were with the Chrysler Research group known as, "Liberty." Here Evan developed computer simulation of hybrid electric vehicles for the corporation. He is named on four patents for hybrid related technology, besides four other patents.

It was at Liberty where he experienced the gathering of misfits. His experience at Chrysler is a unique view; it's from someone who is educated but not in management.